THE HISTORY
of the
KENSINGTON
SOUP SOCIETY

The Kensington Soup Society's Soup House at 1036 Crease Street, east of Wildey Street. *Courtesy of Kensington Soup Society Archives.*

THE HISTORY
of the
KENSINGTON
SOUP SOCIETY

KENNETH W. MILANO

Charleston London

THE
History
PRESS

Published by The History Press
Charleston, SC 29403
www.historypress.net

Copyright © 2009 by Kenneth W. Milano
All rights reserved

All images are courtesy of the author unless otherwise noted.

First published 2009

Manufactured in the United States

ISBN 978.1.59629.624.4

Library of Congress CIP data applied for.

Kensington Soup House.—*This building, located in Allen Street, Eighteenth Ward, daily presents a scene of interest to all who concern themselves about the alleviation of human suffering. The society is now busy in dispensing its charities, and many a crushed spirit is the recipient of its bounty. Every morning hundreds of the poorest residents of the vicinity vie to the spot to have their kettles filled with soup, which is received with an eagerness which shows that want and hunger is pinching. The applicants are of all ages and of both sexes and colors. Ragged children come from squalid homes, but there are also some attired with comparative neatness, who show by their demeanor that their position is strange and unpleasant. Women approach at times timidly, obtain the relief and depart quickly, but with eyes that speak gratitude. Old men bowed with age and sorrow also come, and tearfully thank the dispensers of the nourishment which is to prolong their days of sadness. There is much distress in the vicinity of the Soup House, and the society well deserves the aid and co-operation of the benevolent in their good work.*

—Philadelphia Inquirer, *February 2, 1861*

CONTENTS

ACKNOWLEDGEMENTS

The credit for the creation of this book belongs with the Board of Managers of the Kensington Soup Society. Daniel M. Dailey, one of the managers, first approached me in early 2007 about writing the history of the society. I readily accepted the challenge and would like to publicly thank Dan and the society for putting their trust in my abilities. I would also like to thank the society for putting at my disposal its archives, which helped greatly in the research and writing of this history. Dan was especially helpful in setting up meetings with Soup Society president James D.B. Weiss Jr. at Penn Home and finding the answers to some of the modern-day history questions that troubled me. Dan also read the manuscript and offered helpful insights and needed corrections.

Rich Remer, my cohort in the Kensington History Project, read the entire manuscript and wrote more red ink on it than Sister St. Kevin ever would have back in the early 1970s at St. Anne's. I owe a real big thanks to Rich for helping to edit this manuscript and make sense of it. Of course, any errors and faults will always be my own.

Appreciation also goes out to Jonathan Simcosky of The History Press, who agreed to publish this rather specialized local history book.

John Connors deserves a public thank-you for allowing me to photograph his map of the various Philadelphia soup societies' boundaries.

Last, but certainly not least, thanks are due to my wife Dorina, who puts up with my arcane interests and humors me, and thanks to my sons Francesco and Salvatore, who allowed me from time to time to retreat to the study to write this book.

CHAPTER 1

THE FOUNDING OF THE KENSINGTON SOUP SOCIETY

SHILLING CONCERTS FOR THE POOR—THE EAST KENSINGTON SOUP SOCIETY

On January 29, 1844, the *Philadelphia Public Ledger* ran the following headline on its front page:

> *Shilling Concerts for the Poor.—A Dollar Concert for 19½ Cents!…to be given This Evening, Jan. 29th, 1844, at the Chinese Museum, Great Vocal Attraction; Two Bands on the same Night.*

This headline was the lead story that day, and the concert was the third in a series of weekly benefit concerts for the poor. A previous concert, held the week before, benefited the Seaman's Friend Society; it proved very successful and the series of concerts continued. These benefit concerts saw the entire proceeds of the show go directly to the designated charitable group for that evening.

On this particular January night in the winter of 1844, the "shilling concert" was held for the benefit of a newly organized charity called the East Kensington Soup Society, the forerunner to the present-day Kensington Soup Society.

The concert attendees for this benefit were treated to two bands; first came the popular Captain Herman's celebrated German Brass Band, followed by Francis "Frank" Johnson's Brass and String Band. Frank Johnson (1792–

1844), an innovative composer and bandmaster, was said to have been born in Martinique, in the West Indies, presumably a descendant of slaves. Johnson immigrated to Philadelphia about the year 1809, and by the end of his life he had become the first bandmaster to perform to an integrated audience (circa 1843–44).

This January 29, 1844 benefit concert for the East Kensington Soup Society may very well have been one of those early integrated audiences. Johnson was well known and in great demand in his day. This benefit concert was performed fewer then three months before Johnson's death in April 1844. Johnson's legacy lives on today.

Miss Helen Mathews, a singer and actress of beauty and talent, also performed that night for the East Kensington Soup Society benefit. In her day (the 1840–50s), she appeared across the country in cities as near and far as Philadelphia, Boston, New York, Milwaukee and Cleveland. She may have had a German background, as she worked with many German bands and played in cities with large German populations, but this also might have been due to the popularity at that time of German bands.

Besides the bands and Ms. Mathews, the shilling concert audience for the Soup Society benefit also heard from a number of other vocalists, such as Mrs. Watson, Miss Fanny Ince, Mr. Quayle and Mr. Harrison. All were conducted by one Mr. Watson on a pianoforte furnished by Conrad Meyer, the well-known Philadelphia piano maker. There were also comic songs sung by the veteran Mr. Hadaway (presumably Thomas H. Hadaway) under contract with Ethelbert A. Marshall, who ran both the Broadway Theater in New York and the Walnut Theater in Philadelphia.

The shilling concerts mentioned in the newspaper column were very popular forms of entertainment in the mid-nineteenth century. This East Kensington Soup Society benefit concert was also advertised in the *New York Herald*. J. Warner Erwin, a local Philadelphian, noted in his diary on November 5, 1844, that one such shilling concert he went to had three to four thousand people in attendance. With such a great cast of vocalists and musicians for the Soup Society benefit, one can only imagine that it was quite successful. The proceeds of the concert, perhaps as high as $800, would have helped fund the newly formed organization.

The Chinese Saloon, also known as the Chinese Museum, the place of the benefit concert, was located at the northeast corner of Ninth and Sansom Streets in Philadelphia. This museum could hold upward of 4,500 people for shows. This building was the descendant of the famous Peale's Museum of Charles Willson Peale, later named the Philadelphia Museum. The first floor of the Philadelphia Museum had been dubbed the Chinese Saloon, as it was there that Nathan Dunn's collection of Chinese curiosities was originally displayed between the years 1839 and 1841.

The fact that the Soup Society was first called the East Kensington Soup Society appears to show that the organization may have been formed to benefit the Protestant sections of the then self-governing district. East Kensington was the name given to the area east of Frankford Avenue. The name came into being for political districting reasons. The fact that the benefit concert was advertised as being for the East Kensington Soup Society may signify that the Soup Society, founded by Protestants, some of whom were known Nativists (members of the Native American Party, an anti-Catholic political party), wanted it to be known that the concert was to benefit Protestant East Kensington and not Irish Catholic West Kensington. The fact that it was also advertised in a New York City newspaper, a place where the Nativist Party was born the previous year (1843), is telling as well.

The area in Kensington west of Frankford Avenue, though Protestants did live there, was the area to where large influxes of potato famine Irish Catholics were immigrating in the 1840s. Primary elections in March 1846 show the distinct breakdown of ethnic relations in Kensington. Kensington's first, fourth, fifth and sixth wards (all of the old part of Kensington mainly east of Front Street) took the Nativist ticket, while the second, third and seventh wards (mainly west of Front Street) went to the Democrats.

It is also quite possible that in the early years (1844 to 1853) of the Kensington Soup Society, the official title might very well have been the East Kensington Soup Society, only dropping the "East" from its name when the society was finally incorporated in April 1853. By this time, the Nativist Party had just about peaked in its activities and the excited year of 1844 (the year of the Philadelphia anti- Irish Catholic riots) was almost a decade past, with perhaps the hardcore elements of the local Nativist sympathies starting to die out.

Since the Soup Society was first advertised as the East Kensington Soup Society, it would be good to take a look at just how much involvement, if any, the Nativist movement played in the founding of this organization. Was the original usage of "East" simply because these two areas of Kensington were well-established communities that were extremely aware of their differences before the Nativist controversies of the 1840s? Or did the Nativist political movement play a role in the founding of the organization?

NATIVIST INFLUENCES IN THE FOUNDING OF THE EAST KENSINGTON SOUP SOCIETY

At the time the East Kensington Soup Society was founded in January 1844, America had been seized by the rise of the Know Nothing Party. This was a political movement of American-born Protestants (thus "Nativists") who were fearful of the rising tide of Irish Catholic immigrants flooding American cities in the 1840s due to the Irish potato famine. Originating in New York City in 1843, the American Republican Party was nicknamed the "Know Nothings" and spread to other states as the "Native American Party." The term "Know Nothing" originated in the semi-secrecy surrounding the organization and founding of the party. When a member was questioned about the party activities, he was supposed to reply, "I know nothing."

The Nativists were strengthened by popular fears that the country was being overrun by Irish Catholic immigrants, who were thought to be hostile to American values. They also thought Irish Catholics were controlled by the pope in Rome and that the whole affair was some sort of "popish plot" to take over America. The Nativist movement reached its peak in the mid-1850s in its efforts to stop or at least slow down immigration and naturalization. Eventually, the party fragmented and was absorbed by other political parties of the day.

The Kensington anti–Irish Catholic riots took place in May 1844, in and around American and Masters Streets. American Protestants fought with Irish Catholic immigrants.

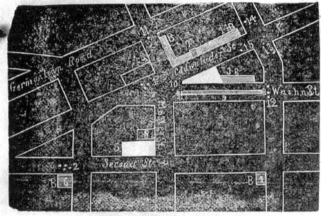

OUTRAGE, RIOTS, AND BLOODSHED !

BURNING OF HOUSES AND CHURCHES.

Men Shot Dead in the Streets !---City and Districts under Martial Law !

Arrival of Gov. Porter, Military from the adjacent Towns, etc. etc

FULL PARTICULAR

KEY TO THE ENGRAVING:

5. Lot where the first meeting was held.
9. The Market House where the meeting adjourned to.
7. Hibernia Hose House, from which the first volley of musketry was fired into the meeting.
10. Open lot across which they fired.
8. Master Street School.
11. Place where Shiffler was shot on Monday afternoon,
6. Seminary.
2. Place where Wright, Ramsey, and others were shot, on Monday night.
1. Place where Grebble, Rinedollar, and others were shot, on Tuesday afternoon.
4. St. Michael's Church.
12. The place where Col. Albright and others were shot.
13. The place where Matthew Hammett was shot.
14. The position from which the boy fired a pistol and shot one of the principal Irish rioters, while he was in the act of firing a musket from the corner marked (15.)
*. The place where Rice (an Irish Catholic) was killed, while in the act of firing, for the third time, on the Native Americans.
B. Blocks of Houses that were burned.

Contemporary broadside showing a map of the Kensington riots of May 1844 around the American and Master Streets area. *Courtesy of Daniel M. Dailey.*

Kensington was a self-governing district within Philadelphia County during the years 1820 to 1854. It had always been a predominantly Protestant area, and during the 1840s, the schools generally began their day with the reading of the Protestant version of scripture, the King James Bible.

However, up in Kensington, large groups of Irish Catholics were moving into the western sections of the district, particularly the third ward. St. Michael's Church, at Second and Master Streets, became the center of Irish life for West Kensington, and the Irish Catholics were not particularly fond of being forced to read Protestant scripture in class.

In November 1842, Philadelphia's Roman Catholic bishop, Francis Kenrick, asked the city's Board of Controllers of the public schools to let Catholic children read from the Douai Bible, the Catholic version of the scriptures. Before the issue could be decided, Kensington's Irish Catholic alderman Hugh Clarke, who was also one of the controllers for the school board, got involved. The reading of scriptures was supposed to have stopped until the issue was settled by the school board; however, when Clarke was visiting a local school in West Kensington, he saw that teachers were still forcing Catholics to read from the King James Bible. Clarke became enraged and stopped the reading of the Bible altogether. The Nativists saw this as a sign that the Catholics were eliminating Bible reading from the schools.

In the months following Bishop Kenrick's request, an anti-Catholic group (the Know Nothings) twisted Bishop Kenrick's request and Clarke's actions around, making them into an attack against the King James Bible and framing them as the invasion of the pope's army. The controversy over which Bible to read in the public schools excited the people. Anti-Catholic and Nativist groups held meetings in various lots and halls. In Kensington in early March 1844 (two months after the benefit concert for the Soup Society), a mass meeting was held at Comissioner's Hall. The hall served as Kensington's city hall and was located at Frankford Road and Master Street. It was reported by the *North American and Daily Advertiser* that the meeting attracted 2,500 people, with as many forced to stand outside the hall, as the crowd exceeded the hall's capacity.

The meeting was filled with anti-Catholic speeches. H.A. Salter assisted Thomas J. Taylor as the presiding officer and George App, Esq., chaired the meeting. The meeting featured several speakers, including the attorney E.D. Tarr, conveyancer H.A. Salter, Alderman Peter Rambo, Thos. J. Taylor, Abraham P. Eyre (wharf builder and one-time president of the District of Kensington), John Painter and a host of Protestant ministers: Reverends Ketchum, Webster, Burg and Inskip.

Reverend Inskip was a minister at Kensington Methodist Episcopal "Old Brick" Church. He served this church in the early years of the 1840s, before moving on to western Pennsylvania for his next appointment. This charismatic minister of Kensington was probably the inspiration for the

Commissioner's Hall during Kensington's self-governing period (1820–54), northwest corner Frankford Avenue and Master Street. It was here that the Nativists rallied in March 1844.

Reverend John S. Inskip (1816–1884), a minister at Kensington Methodist Episcopal "Old Brick" Church, helped to flame the rage during the riots of 1844.

founding of the Soup Society. He also appears to have been a hardcore Nativist—the following excerpt of his speech at this Nativist meeting drew loud applause:

> *That we view the recent efforts of the Roman Catholics, of this and other cities, to abolish the use of the Bible in our public schools, as a sure indication that the church of Rome continues to grasp after unauthorized power, and designs to take from us rights, for the preservation of which we count no sacrifice too great; and that to guard these rights, and perpetuate them unimpaired to our children and succeeding generations, we here pledge our property, our influence, our prayers, our lives and our sacred honor.*

H.A. Salter, who helped to run the meeting, offered the following comments in his speech:

> *That this meeting do recommend to the citizens of this community, the favorable notice and patronage of the* Philadelphia North American; *and* Daily Sun *published by L.C. Levin, Esq., as papers deserving the encouragement of every Protestant and lover of liberty. That this meeting pledge themselves, both individually and collectively, to oppose the re-election of any of the present Board of Commissioners, who may hereafter vote for Hugh Clark for School Director, or any other office within their gift.*

Fired by the Nativists during the Kensington riots of May 1844, the Nanny Goat Market, Irish homes and the Hibernia Hose Company went up in flames.

18

The Founding of the Kensington Soup Society

The smoldering ruins of the Nanny Goat Market and Irish Catholic homes, American Street, north of Master Street, facing west.

Salter, in his speech, instructed the crowd to support L.C. Levin, the man who two months later, in May 1844, was one of the central figures who incited the anti–Irish Catholic riots in Kensington. When the riots broke out, St. Michael's Church (a Catholic church), as well as its convent, was burned to the ground. Blocks of Irish Catholic homes along Cadwalader and Master Streets and the local Hibernia Fire Hose Company were also fired and lost. The local Nanny Goat Market, opposite the fire hose company, was burned. There were also a number of people killed and wounded. One has to wonder if the fiery speech of Reverend Inskip, who told people to pledge their property, their influence, their prayers, their lives and their sacred honor, did not help to excite the Protestant mobs of Kensington.

Salter, a Nativist Party legislator in the Pennsylvania Statehouse the following September, was also one of the early managers of the Kensington Soup Society. While not mentioned as being at this March Nativist meeting, Jacob Tees, another early Soup Society manager, was also elected on the Nativist ticket with Salter and served as a Pennsylvania state representative for Kensington.

There were also two other early officers of the Soup Society who attended this March Nativist meeting: future president of the society Abraham P. Eyre (who was also a one-time president of the Board of Commissioners of Kensington) spoke to the mob, and George J. Hamilton, the longtime treasurer of the Kensington Soup Society, was noted to have attended this Nativist rally.

In the surviving notes and records of the Kensington Soup Society, it is stated that the society was founded in 1844, the same year as the Nativist meeting described above, which leads one to wonder under what circumstances the Soup Society was founded. Could it be that the men who founded the Soup Society were inspired to help their fellow men in need, regardless of religion? Or were they inspired to help only fellow Protestants in need? Was the founding of the Soup Society a way to do outreach work among the Protestant poor, perhaps as a way to make sure they stayed within the Protestant faith?

The fact that two early officers of the Soup Society and two other managers of the Soup Society were reported to have attended a major Nativist meeting in March 1844 shows that the Soup Society had officers that were Nativists. A charismatic and inspirational minister who more likely than not helped to inspire local Kensingtonians to found the Soup Society was also present and very active at the March 1844 Nativist meeting.

For whatever underlying reasons the Kensington Soup Society was founded, it is clear that the immediate needs of the people of Kensington were certainly uppermost in the minds of the society's founders. The Panic of 1837, one of the worst economic depressions in the history of America, had left many Kensingtonians jobless and desperate, and its effects were still present in 1844. Kensington responded with the founding of the Soup Society.

KENSINGTON METHODIST EPISCOPAL CHURCH AND THE KENSINGTON SOUP SOCIETY

From what little evidence remains of those early years of the founding of the Soup Society, it is clear that the Kensington Methodist Episcopal "Old Brick" Church was instrumental in the society's founding. Eleven of the founding members of the Soup Society also served as trustees of Old Brick in the early years of the Soup Society (pre-1860): John Vaughan, Matthias Creamer, Jacob Tees, George J. Hamilton, Andrew Zane, Joseph Lippincott, Joseph Bennett, Theodore Birely, David Duncan, Thomas D. Stites and Franklin Eyre. Later in the nineteenth century there were A.H. McFadden, George Kessler and I.P.H. Wilmerton. Henry Kessler, who served as a trustee of Old Brick in the 1830s, also served on the Soup Society board after its founding.

The Founding of the Kensington Soup Society

Kensington ME "Old Brick" Church, Richmond and Marlborough Streets. Many of the trustees of this church were also managers of the Soup Society.

Also among the "class leaders" of Old Brick at the time of the organization and incorporation of the Kensington Soup Society, you will find there are no fewer than five (Matthias Creamer, Joseph Lippincott, Franklin Eyre, Joseph Bennett and George J. Hamilton) who were also founders of the Soup Society. Factor into the equation the probably related family members of Old Brick class leaders (William S. Zane, John Kessler, William Bennett and John Bennett) and the Soup Society founders and the numbers would increase.

In June 1843, Old Brick Church amended its original constitution. Of the nine trustees of the church that signed their names to the document in January 1844, five were founding directors of the Soup Society (John Vaughan, Matthias Creamer, George J. Hamilton, Joseph Lippincott and Andrew Zane). Another, Henry Kessler, would later serve on the board of the Soup Society, and at least one other, William Bennett, was probably a family member of Soup Society founders.

Given the similar makeup of their founding members, it would appear that the Soup Society may have been a charitable effort on the part of Old Brick Church. The fact that the Board of Managers of the Soup Society had their annual meetings at Old Brick in its early years would also seem to point

This lot is where 208 Allen Street was once located. This was the original home of the Kensington Soup Society for the years 1844 to 1863. Today it is a parking lot.

in this direction. Shortly after incorporation of the Soup Society (1853), Old Brick erected its new church building (1854).

The Methodists were very keen to preach the gospel to the poor. In 1840–41, Old Brick's Sunday School Association had as its officers Matthias Creamer, superintendent; Henry Kessler, treasurer; George J. Hamilton, secretary; and Joseph Bennett, librarian. All of these men had connections to the Soup Society. Creamer, Kessler, Hamilton and Bennett were either founders, officers or managers of the Soup Society, while Creamer's daughter, Catharine Creamer, was the wife of Joseph Bennett, another founder of the society.

When it came time to construct a new church for Old Brick, the Building Committee consisted of George J. Hamilton, president and treasurer; Reverend P. Coombe, secretary; and Franklin Eyre, Joseph Bennett and David Duncan. Except for Reverend Coombe, all of these men were founders of the Soup Society.

With much overlapping of the board of trustees of Old Brick and the founding board of the Soup Society, one might wonder if the charismatic minister of that time at Old Brick, Reverend John S. Inskip (1816–1884), may have had something to do with the founding of the Soup Society?

The Founding of the Kensington Soup Society

Catharine Bennett, born Catharine Creamer, was the wife of Joseph Bennett, a Soup Society founder, and the daughter of another founder, Matthias Creamer.

Inskip was born in Huntingdon, England, and came to America with his parents when he was only four years old. The family settled in Wilmington, Delaware. In 1832, he converted to the Methodist Church and in 1835 was licensed by them to preach. By 1838, he had been ordained a deacon in Wilmington. After serving on several circuits, he was ordained an elder in Philadelphia in 1840, and in 1842 he was appointed to Kensington ME Old Brick Church, where he stayed for two years.

Inskip was described as a man of "great energy, a strong preacher, a born reformer." During his two years at Old Brick (1842–43, the two years leading up to the founding of the Soup Society in 1844), the membership of Old Brick rose from 540 in 1841 when he came to 600 in 1842, and then to 700 members in 1843, an increase of 160 members in two years! Inskip's autobiography (published in a memorial when he died) states that 300 people were converted while he was at Kensington.

After Philadelphia, Inskip served in Ohio, New York and Maryland. He was one of the founders of the National Camp Meeting Association and is credited with being involved in the first distinct Holiness Camp Meeting in 1867, in Vineland, New Jersey, which led to the founding of the "Tent City" at Ocean Grove, New Jersey, where he died in 1884. During his lifetime, he had become president of the National Camp Meeting Association and the editor of the *Christian Standard*. He was known worldwide and is considered the Billy Graham of his day.

While the official church history (Swindell's *Annals of Kensington Methodist Episcopal Church*) does not mention the Kensington Soup Society, it would be hard to imagine, with all of these overlapping board members, that Kensington's Old Brick Church did not have something to do with the founding of the Soup Society.

In one of the speeches published in his memorial (*Memorial of Rev. John S. Inskip*), the Philadelphia Preacher's Meeting had this to say about Reverend Inskip:

> *His ability as a preacher, decided views on great moral questions in Church and State, courage and boldness in the advocacy of his convictions, power and skill in the organization of large masses of people for direct spiritual results, zeal in the promulgation of the doctrine of holiness, in these and other lands.*

One of the signatories for this piece was Reverend W. Swindells, the succeeding minister of Kensington's Old Brick Church, who wrote the history of the church in 1893.

Swindell's piece mentions that Reverend Inskip's abilities helped to decide great moral questions in church and state. He may have been alluding to the time (mentioned previously) in March 1844 when, at a mass meeting in Kensington, Inskip roused the crowd with a speech on the issue of reading the Bible in public schools. In two months' time, this issue would be the catalyst for the explosion of Kensington's anti–Irish Catholic riots in May 1844, and the resulting loss of life and property.

OVERLAPPING BOARDS OF DIRECTORS OF THE KENSINGTON SOUP SOCIETY

As might be expected in a tightknit community like Kensington, a number of the members of the early Board of Managers of the Soup Society worked together in the founding of other Kensington institutions. Besides the overlapping boards for the Kensington ME Church and the Kensington Soup Society, another instance of overlap with the Soup Society was the Kensington Building Association. Founded in 1847, this association was considered the "father of building associations." While not the first (that honor goes to a group of Englishmen in Frankford, Pennsylvania, in 1837), the Kensington Building Association was the most successful and the model was copied across the state to the point that in 1884, there were 233 associations in Philadelphia and nearly 1,000 in Pennsylvania.

The "building associations" proper, which had done so much to make Philadelphia a city of homes, were really not building societies at all, but cooperative banking associations making loans on land and houses to their members. From the Philadelphia newspaper, the *North American*, of February 11, 1847, we find a number of the Kensington Soup Society's early officers and managers also involved in the founding of the Kensington Building Association. It almost reads like a who's who of the founders of the Kensington Soup Society:

> *At an adjourned meeting of the Kensington Building Association, held "pursuant to public notice," at the Hall of the Kensington Engine Company—A.P. Eyre, President, in the Chair, and S.F. Hay, Secretary—after the reading and adoption of the minutes of the previous meeting and disposition of preliminary business, the roll of Subscribers was called, when it appeared that 207 shares had been disposed of, and initiation fees to the amount of $306 were collected.*
>
> *On motion, it was Resolved, That the Association do now permanently organize by the election of Officers for the ensuing year.*
>
> *The following gentlemen were duly elected managers viz; A.P. Eyre, P.F. Wright, Wm. Cramp, Joseph Smith, Jacob Jones, Ralph Lee, Joseph Bennett, George W. Vaughan, Hillman Troth,*
>
> *On the same evening, at a meeting of the Board of Directors, Abraham P. Eyre was elected President, and H.A. Salter, Secretary, and Edward W. Gorgas, Treasurer* [extract from the minutes] *H.A. Salter, Sec'ry.*
>
> *N.B. There will be an adjoined meeting held at the Kensington Engine House, on Friday Evening, the 12th inst., at 7 o'clock.*

No fewer than seven founders of the Kensington Building Association were also founders or early managers of the Kensington Soup Society: A.P. Eyre, William Cramp, Jacob Jones, Joseph Bennett, George W. Vaughan, H.A. Salter and Edward W. Gorgas.

Only seven years later, in 1854, a year after the incorporation of the Kensington Soup Society, the Kensington Mutual Fire and Marine Insurance Company was incorporated. Eleven of the incorporators of this insurance company were either incorporators of the Kensington Soup Society or early members of its Board of Managers. Those eleven from the Board of Managers were Henry Bumm, George J. Hamilton, Edward W. Gorgas, Charles M. Lukens, H.A. Salter, John P. Verree, John H. Bringhurst, Abraham P. Eyre, Jacob Jones, William Albertson and Peter Fisher.

The boards of directors for the Kensington ME Church, the Kensington Building Association, the Kensington Mutual Fire and Marine Insurance Company and still later the Kensington National Bank all had many overlapping members with the Board of Managers of the Kensington Soup Society. Truly, the founders and early managers of the Kensington Soup Society were the integral leaders and builders of the Kensington community.

CHAPTER 2

THE EARLY YEARS OF THE SOUP
SOCIETY—MANAGERS AND BENEFACTORS

EARLIEST KNOWN MANAGERS AND OFFICERS OF THE
KENSINGTON SOUP SOCIETY, 1844–74

The earliest ledger of the minutes of the Kensington Soup Society's meetings that has survived begins on November 19, 1875. There are several loose sheets of paper with meeting minutes for the late 1860s that survived separately, as well as notes from a single meeting of 1859. If there had been an actual ledger for the society previous to this November 19, 1875 date, it would have presumably covered the period of 1844 (when the society was organized) through to the fall of 1875, when the surviving ledgers start. The loose sheets that have survived from prior to the fall of 1875 appear to be pieces of paper where meeting notes were jotted down and later transferred into a ledger book. They are not pages torn from a previous "unknown" ledger.

While there are loose sheets from the 1860s and some letterhead of various vendors that the society dealt with in the 1860s, no documents have survived from the first decade of the Kensington Soup Society (1844–54), except for a copy of the 1854 publication of the society's constitution, bylaws and officers.

If we examine the *Constitution, By Laws, and Officers of the Kensington Soup Society, in the County of Philadelphia* printed in 1854, we find that the Board of Managers for that year differs from the Board of Managers that is listed in a 1912 reprinting of the *Constitution, By-Laws, and Officers.* The 1912 publication

Philadelphia's Laurel Hill Cemetery, burial place of the wealthy. Thirteen founders of the Kensington Soup Society are buried here. *Courtesy of Laurel Hill Cemetery.*

lists the original incorporators of April 18, 1853. Therefore, from the time of the incorporation of the society in April 1853 and the printing of the constitution, bylaws and officers in 1854, there was possibly a change in the Board of Managers of four individuals, as seen below in Table 1.

TABLE 1. Comparison of the 1854 and 1912 printings of Soup Society's constitution and bylaws, listing the original incorporators of the society and showing that 1912 has four extra incorporators (shown in **bold** type).

Board of Managers of the Kensington Soup Society Constitution, Bylaws and Officers, Philadelphia: 1854	Board of Managers of the Kensington Soup Society listed in Articles of Incorporation April 18, 1853, Philadelphia: 1912
Andrew Zane	Andrew Zane
G.J. Hamilton	G.J. Hamilton
Joseph Lippincott	Joseph Lippincott

Joseph Bennett	Joseph Bennett
Robert Pearce	Robert Pearce
Jacob K. Vaughan	Jacob K. Vaughan
	John Clouds
Abraham P. Eyre	Abraham P. Eyre
Thos. D. Stites	Thomas D. Stites
	Jos. P. Cramer
Eli Garrison Sr.	Eli Garrison Sr.
Franklin Eyre	Franklin Eyre
Jacob Tees	Jacob Tees
	George S. Cox
David Duncan	David Duncan
	Jacob P. Donaldson
George W. Vaughan	George W. Vaughan
Edward H. Gorgas	Edward H. Gorgas
Jeheu Eyre	Jeheu Eyre
Theodore Birely	Theodore Birely
Jacob Jones	Jacob Jones
William Cramp	Wm. Cramp
George Stockham	George Stockham
Richard S. Allen	Richard S. Allen

The two lists are identical in the order of the printing of the names; however, the 1854 list has four fewer individuals: John Clouds, Jos. P. Cramer, George S. Cox and Jacob P. Donaldson. Why the two lists differ is unclear. It could be that the incorporating Board of Managers simply had four additional members and a year later the board was shortened, or perhaps the incorporators included all those involved in the society and not just the Board of Managers, and it was from the 1853 list of twenty-four individuals that the twenty-member 1854 Board of Managers was elected.

In a volume titled *Laws of the General Assembly of the Commonwealth of Pennsylvania Passed at the Session of 1853*, we find, "An Act to incorporate the

The structure at 313 Richmond Street was the family home of one of the Soup Society's founders, Theodore Birely, a famed Kensington shipbuilder. *Courtesy of Daniel M. Dailey.*

The burial plot of the family of Jacob Tees (1789–1875), founder of the Soup Society, sits in Palmer Cemetery, aka the Kensington Burial Grounds.

Kensington Soup Society, in the county of Philadelphia." In Section 1 of Act No. 305, we find a list of not twenty-four, but twenty-five names of men who are stated to have been the incorporators of the Kensington Soup Society. Besides the above-listed twenty-four names, there is the additional name of Matthias Cramer. Since this act of the Pennsylvania legislature would appear to be the "official" document for the list of names of the incorporators, the reprint of the constitution and bylaws of 1912 appears to be in error by one name.

While these two printed publications of the Kensington Soup Society (1854 constitution printing and 1912 reprint) and the Pennsylvania legislature's *Laws of the General Assembly* give us an idea of the Board of Managers for the period of 1853–54, the availability of meeting minutes still come up short for the period between 1844 and 1853 and for the period between 1854 and 1873–74, when an annual report was published that lists the Board of Managers and officers. For the period from 1854 to 1873, we have to look at old newspaper notices or other ephemeral matter that has survived to see who served on the Board of Managers.

Matthias Creamer (1787–1853) was one of the founders of the Kensington Soup Society, father-in-law of founder Joseph Bennett and brother-in-law to another founder, John Vaughan.

Jacob Keen Vaughan (1812–1886) was the son of John Vaughan. He and his father, both shipbuilders, were also founders of the Kensington Soup Society.

The Early Years of the Soup Society—Managers and Benefactors

The Kensington Soup Society is not found in the Philadelphia city directories during the period of 1844 to 1859. The Philadelphia directories prior to 1854 were not that thorough for the district of Kensington. In 1854, the whole of the county of Philadelphia was incorporated into the city of Philadelphia, and it was then more normal for Kensington to be canvassed by the publishers of the city directories.

In McElroy's Philadelphia city directory of 1860, we find the first mention of the Kensington Soup Society. The directory states that the society was located on Shackamaxon Street. Robert Clark was listed as president, Jacob Keen Vaughan as secretary and George J. Hamilton as treasurer. However, Cohen's Philadelphia city directory for the same year shows Abraham P. Eyre as president. Obviously something was slightly off kilter or perhaps some sort of printing error occurred.

Another check of McElroy's directory for 1860 shows a Robert Clark as president of the Southwark Soup Society, which may be the root of the possible error, since it is rather doubtful that Robert Clark would be president of both the Southwark Soup Society and the Kensington Soup Society. Searching for Robert Clark in the city directory listings shows several likely Robert Clarks to be a match, with the most likely being a lumberman from Southwark. There is no Robert Clark in the Kensington area. Abraham P. Eyre was the president of the Kensington Soup Society in 1854 as well as in 1861–62, so he presumably would have been the president as well in 1860.

Since meeting minutes do not exist before 1875, we can check the Philadelphia city directories for hints of the officers of the society for the years 1861 to 1875. Abraham P. Eyre was president in 1861–62 and George Stockham was president from 1863 to 1872. John Robbins held the presidency for the years 1873 to 1875. The secretary was Jacob Keen Vaughan in 1861 and Charles M. Lukens from 1862 to 1875 (although his name is misprinted in the directory of 1873–75). George J. Hamilton remained treasurer from 1861 to 1875; he may have also served as secretary in 1871–72, unless the directory was a misprint. The vice-president was only mentioned in the directories of 1871–75, when Edward W. Gorgas held that office.

When the Kensington Soup Society first appeared in Philadelphia city directories in 1860, the address was given as Shackamaxon Street, where it remained until the directory of 1862, when the address was listed as 208 Allen Street. In the directory of 1869, it was listed as being at 247 Allen Street. The directories state that the society stayed at that address (which was less than a block north from the first address) until it appeared in the directory of 1874 at 1036 Crease Street, although the first few years the directory misprinted the address as 1936 Crease Street.

The city directories were generally compiled at the end of the preceding year; thus, if the Kensington Soup Society appears in the 1869 city directory listed at 247 Allen Street, it would mean that the society had moved there by late 1868. However, the people who compiled the city directories sometimes relied on information they had compiled the previous year. It would appear that the entire city was not canvassed every year, but only certain listings or entries, as the Philadelphia city directories (as listed above) show the Kensington Soup Society moving to its 247 Allen Street address in about the years 1868–69, when in fact the *Philadelphia Inquirer* newspaper had published notices by the year 1864 stating that the Kensington Soup Society was already at 247 Allen Street.

While the city directories do not give us all of the members of the Board of Managers of the Soup Society, they do provide us with the various addresses of the Soup House, as well as the officers of the society. Abraham P. Eyre appears to have been the president of the Soup Society for at least the years 1854 to 1862, at which time George Stockham took over the position, serving from 1863 to 1872. In 1873, the Honorable John Robbins was elected to the presidency and served in that capacity through the 1880 season.

In 1854, Eli Garrison Sr. was vice-president, a post that we do not know if he held during the period of 1860 to 1870, as the city directories did not list this office for those years. However, we do know from 1861 and 1862 newspaper articles that he was the vice-president in those years, so he would have probably held the position for at least the years 1854 to 1862. There is also one loose sheet document from the Soup Society's archives that exists from a meeting on December 26, 1867, showing Eli Garrison attending the meeting. There is no mention that he is the vice-president, but tradition would show that once elected to an officer position, an individual generally kept that position until he retired from the Board of Managers, moved to another officer position or died.

An article alerting the public of the elections results for the Board of Managers of the Kensington Soup Society published in the *North American & United States Gazette* of December 18, 1867, shows Eli Garrison elected to the board for the 1867–68 season. We can assume that he held the vice-president's office for the season of 1867–68, as we do have proof of him holding that office the previous season (1866–67). We are then left with only the three seasons of 1868–69, 1869–70 and 1870–71 in which it is not clear

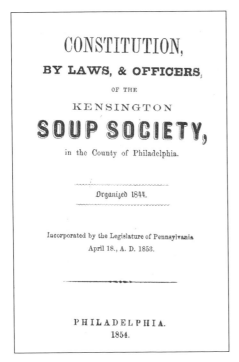

CONSTITUTION,

BY LAWS, & OFFICERS,

OF THE

KENSINGTON

SOUP SOCIETY,

in the County of Philadelphia.

Organized 1844.

Incorporated by the Legislature of Pennsylvania
April 18., A. D. 1853.

PHILADELPHIA.
1854.

The oldest document that survives in the Kensington Soup Society's archives is this original 1854 printed pamphlet of the society's constitution, bylaws and officers. *Kensington Soup Society Archives.*

whether Garrison or Gorgas was the vice-president. However, from articles found in the *Philadelphia Inquirer* stating that Garrison was elected to the Board of Managers in December 1869, for the 1869–70 season, we can assume he was also on the Board of Managers for the 1868–69 season and thus we can also assume that he kept his vice-president's position for both of these seasons.

An obituary for Garrison published in the *Philadelphia Inquirer* on August 29, 1870, tells us that Garrison died on August 25, which indicates that he would have missed being on the Board of Managers for the season of 1870–71. Thus, Edward W. Gorgas took over the office of vice-president in that year.

The 1854 constitution and bylaws publication lists Jacob K. Vaughan as the secretary of the Soup Society; he served in this position until 1861, when Charles M. Lukens took over and remained the secretary until 1899.

George J. Hamilton, who was from an old Kensington family, served as treasurer of the Soup Society. Hamilton was a banker by profession and served as treasurer from 1854 to 1882.

Among the records that have survived over the years for the Soup Society, only one document prior to 1875 records an Annual Contributors Meeting of the Soup Society, when managers and officers were being elected. There are newspaper reports about the annual meetings for the decade of the 1860s and the early 1870s, but actual documents created by the Soup Society themselves do not exist for the years previous to the fall of 1875. The one record that exists is for a meeting that was held on December 30, 1859. The board elected that day consisted of the following twenty-five men:

A.P. Eyre	E. Garrison	S. McCutchen
John Robbins Jr.	Geo. J. Hamilton	A. Zane
J.H. Bringhurst	H.J. Worrall	Jacob Jones
Richard Wainwright	Geo. Stockham	E.W. Gorgas
Chas. Lukens	J.K. Vaughan	D. Duncan
H.[A.] Salter	Thos D. Stites	Wm. Albertson
Jos. Gillingham	Charles Thomas	G.W. Vaughan
Chas Ruffell	Robert Coleman	H. Bumm
Jos. Paxson		

Abraham P. Eyre was elected president, Eli Garrison vice-president, J.K. Vaughan secretary and George J. Hamilton treasurer. While Eyre, Garrison and Vaughan all received eight votes each, Hamilton only got seven, which meant that his election as treasurer was not unanimous.

This 1859 Board of Managers contains eleven members from the 1854 printed list of the Board of Managers: Andrew Zane, G.J. Hamilton, Jacob K. Vaughan, Abraham P. Eyre, Thomas D. Stites, Eli Garrison Sr., David Duncan, George W. Vaughan, Edward H. Gorgas, Jacob Jones and George Stockham. While the Board of Managers had changed over the course of five years, there was still a core group of eleven members left from the original incorporators of the society.

After the Philadelphia city directories and the above-mentioned 1859 meeting document, the next available document is a list of the Board of Managers of the Kensington Soup Society published as an advertisement for the election results of the Soup Society in the *Philadelphia Inquirer* on January 7, 1861. That full advertisement is as follows:

7 January 1861, Philadelphia Inquirer, *Page 5.*

Kensington Soup Society. At a meeting of citizens, held this evening, January 4, 1861, at the Methodist Episcopal Church, southeast corner of Richmond street and Marlborough street., the following named gentlemen were elected Officers and Managers of the "Kensington Soup Society" for the ensuing year:

Officers. Col. A.P. Eyre.
Vice President, Eli Garrison.
Secretary, Charles M. Lukens.
Treasurer, George J. Hamilton.

Shipbuilder Jacob Birely (1821–1895) briefly sat on the Soup Society's Board of Managers. His brother Theodore was one of the founders of the society. *Courtesy of Daniel M. Dailey.*

Managers.

Col. Abraham P. Eyre	*Eli Garrison*
Samuel M. Mecutchen	*Hon. John Robbins*
George J. Hamilton	*Andrew Zane*
Col. John H. Bringhurst	*Hugh J. Worrall*
Jacob Jones	*Richard Wainwright*
George Stockham	*James Bell*
Charles M. Lukens	*Joseph F.N. Snyder*
David Duncan	*Benjamin H. Brown*
Thomas D. Stites	*Edward W. Gorgas*
Joseph E. Gillingham	*Jacob Birely*
Frederick Creamer	*Henry Kessler*
George W. Vaughan	*Jacob K. Vaughan*
Robert Coleman	

Mr. Daniel B. Mickle was duly elected Agent and Collector for the Society for the ensuing year.

Subscriptions in aid of the Society are respectfully solicited, and may be left with the Treasurer, Mr. George J. Hamilton, at the Commonwealth Bank, S.W. corner of Fourth and Chestnut streets, and other Officers and Managers. Charles M. Lukens, Secretary

If we examine the Board of Directors for 1854, 1859 and 1861, we find that the same eleven members from 1854 who were on the board in 1859 are still serving in 1861: Andrew Zane, G.J. Hamilton, Jacob K. Vaughan, Abraham P. Eyre, Thomas D. Stites, Eli Garrison Sr., David Duncan, George W. Vaughan, Edward H. Gorgas, Jacob Jones and George Stockham.

On the 1859 and 1861 Board of Managers lists, the name Edward W. Gorgas appears instead of the Edward H. Gorgas listed from 1853 and 1854. This would appear to be the same person with a simple typo of the middle initial. While Theodore Birely is no longer on the board in 1861, there is a Jacob Birely, his brother, who had joined the board. Franklin Eyre also is no longer a member in 1861, but his presumed brother Abraham P. Eyre is still the president. Joseph P. Cramer is no longer with the society in 1861, but Frederick Creamer, a presumed relative, has joined. While the Board of Managers gained fifteen new members over the course of seven years (1854 to 1861), it still had a core group of eleven of the original incorporators of the Soup Society to help usher it into the Civil War era.

A review of the available documents for the first three decades of the Soup Society, the thirty years before the meeting minutes ledgers start in 1875, would result in the officers for the Soup Society's earliest years as follows:

President: Abraham P. Eyre, 1854–62; George Stockham, 1862–72; Honorable John Robbins, 1872–80
Vice-president: Eli Garrison Sr., 1854–70; Edward W. Gorgas, 1870–80
Secretary: Jacob K. Vaughan, 1854–61; Charles M. Lukens, 1861–99
Treasurer: George J. Hamilton, 1854–82

Beck and Mercier Bequests—Kensington Soup Society in Context

Prior to the opening of the Kensington Soup Society, the nearest soup house would have been the Northern Soup Society, located at Fourth and Coates (Fairmont) Streets in 1843, with a service list of 2,200 people for that year.

Edward W. Gorgas School, southwest corner of Susquehanna Avenue and Belgrade Street. Gorgas, a school board representative for the eighteenth ward, was also a Soup Society president.

Dr. Abraham Ernest Helffenstein served thirty-three years on the Soup Society's board. His grandfather was shipbuilder John Vaughan, a founder of the society.

The Spring Garden Soup Society was located at Eleventh and Callowhill. In March 1843, both the Northern Soup Society and the Southwark Soup Society were reported very low in funding and their services were much restricted. The winter of 1842–43 had been very bitter and the aid to the poor was much more in need. Even the Southern Soup Society at 16 Green's Court (between Spruce and Pine, Fourth and Fifth Streets) reported the people being in much distress that winter. The Southern Society supplied 31,222 quarts of soup and over 10,500 loaves of bread to 2,580 people at a cost of over $1,100. The entire city and county was still suffering from the Panic of 1837.

It would appear that the demand on the existing soup societies was so great during the winter of 1842–43 that a need was seen for additional soup societies to be created. It must be remembered that at this time (the early 1840s), in addition to the city trying to settle itself from the Panic of 1837, Philadelphia also began seeing an increasing influx of emigrants from the hard times in Ireland leading up to the famine of 1845. Many of these emigrants were extremely destitute.

A number of philanthropic gentlemen of the district of Moyamensing were reported in January 1844 to be trying to establish a soup society in that area just south of the city central. They hosted a lecture on North American Indians, to be given by Colonel McKenney, in the hopes of raising funds. The Moyamensing Soup Society was soon founded, opening for business at Ninth and Shippen (Bainbridge) Streets. An appeal for aid in the winter of 1846 was reported in the press due to the "extreme severity of the weather [that] has caused an increased demand to an extent not before known."

The same month that the Moyamensing Soup Society had its benefit lecture, the East Kensington Soup Society had its benefit concert at the Chinese Saloon. When Paul Beck died in late 1844 and left money to the "Corporation of Philadelphia in aid of Soup Societies," it is probable that the newly founded East Kensington Soup Society saw some of this funding, as did the newly formed Moyamensing Soup Society. The money was to come from the $500 per annum ground rent at 60 Market Street, a place apparently owned by Paul Beck.

The Moyamensing, Southwark, Spring Garden, Western, Northern and Southern Soup Societies all appear in various advertisements posted in the *North American and United States Gazette* during the mid- to late 1840s and into the 1850s. However, the Kensington Soup Society does not appear in any advertisements of this paper. This might be due to the fact that prior to 1854, Kensington was not part of the city of Philadelphia. While Moyamensing,

Northern, Southwark and Spring Garden Soup Societies were also located outside of the city proper prior to 1854, they were adjacent to the core of the city. Kensington, on the other hand, was farther from the city than any of the other soup societies, and thus those adjacent soup societies would have seen more coverage of their activities by the Philadelphia newspapers.

In the Kensington Soup Society's 1854 printed *Constitution, By Laws, & Officers*, there is mentioned the bequest of Charles Mercier. George J. Hamilton, the Soup Society's treasurer, made a special note of the bequest:

> [We] *took pleasure in acknowledging the receipt of One Thousand Dollars from Mr. Valentine Burkart, Executor of the last Will of Charles Mercier, deceased, being the amount of the Legacy left by Mr. Mercier to this Society; and the prompt payment of which is gratefully remembered by the board of Managers.*

It could very well be that bequest of $1,000 helped the Kensington Soup Society's Board of Managers in their decision to finally incorporate. It is generally accepted that the Kensington Soup Society was founded in 1844, but it was only incorporated on April 18, 1853, at about the time of Mercier's bequest.

Charles Mercier died April 27, 1852, and his will was probated on May 3, 1852. His will directed that the treasurers of all soup societies in existence at the time of his death (in Philadelphia) be given $1,000 each, in addition to bequests to St. John's Lutheran Church ($2,000), Zion Lutheran Church ($2,000), the Pennsylvania Bible Society ($3,000), the Missionary Society of St. John's Lutheran ($2,000), Lodge 3 Masonic Brethren ($3,000) and the Union Benevolent Society ($5,000).

Since treasurer Hamilton thanked the executor of Mercier's estate for a "prompt payment," we can assume that the Soup Society received the $1,000 bequest sometime in the fall or winter of 1852, which means it would have been received just before the Soup Society formally incorporated in April 1853. The bequest, in all probability, helped the managers of the society with their decision to incorporate, as they now had at least $1,000 in their treasury.

Charles Mercier was a confectioner who lived at 111 South Third Street. After a successful twenty-year career in the business, he retired in 1826 and devoted the rest of his life to local politics and philanthropy.

With the help of Charles Mercier's bequest and the formal incorporation in 1853, the Kensington Soup Society became part of a citywide network of soup societies. While the above-mentioned research has helped for the most part to figure out who the early officers and Board of Managers of the society were and how the society came to be founded, we are still left to determine just how the society functioned during those early years when records do not exist (circa 1844–75).

The first mention of the Kensington Soup Society appears in the *North American and United States Gazette* (*NA and U.S. Gazette*) on February 14, 1857, where it is noted that it, along with six other soup societies, all received ten dollars each from Minnehaha Lodge No. 1 of Pennsylvania, of the Independent Order of the Sons of Malta. On March 9, 1858, the *North American and United States Gazette* ran the following article:

> *The Nineteenth Ward.—The suffering in this vicinity, to which we recently directed attention, calls for further relief. No aid has been furnished and benevolent individuals in that section have been taxed to the uttermost. The Kensington Soup Society, which since December last, has been feeding some 240 families, in all about 1100 persons, is out of funds, and is compelled to make a fresh appeal for assistance. Any contributions intended for its use may be sent to A.P. Eyre, the President, or J.K. Vaughan, the Secretary, through the Kensington post office; or if left with us will be promptly and properly forwarded.*

The next notice of the Kensington Soup Society is in the *NA and U.S. Gazette* on January 10, 1859, when it was stated that the Independent Order of the Sons of Malta distributed five hundred tickets to the Kensington Soup Society (as it did to all of the other soup societies), each ticket retrievable for a loaf of bread from one of the soup societies.

While the registers of the Kensington Soup Society are missing prior to November 1875, there exist various registers of minutes for other soup societies in the city of Philadelphia. By reviewing these other society minutes, we can get a glimmer of information or infer some observations about the Kensington Soup Society.

At a meeting of the Spring Garden Soup Society, held on November 18, 1857, various delegates from six soup societies met for the setting of boundaries for their respective service areas. The necessity of setting boundaries had become an issue ever since the consolidation of Philadelphia County into the city of Philadelphia took place in 1854. The six soup societies and the boundaries they created were as follows:

Southwark Soup Society: Sutherland Street below Queen Street, east of Second Street; lower side of Shippen (Bainbridge) Street, east of Broad Street.

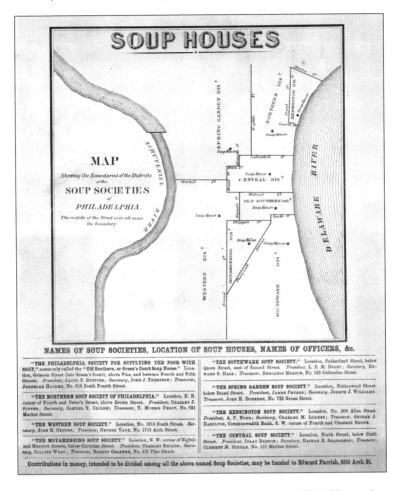

Map of the boundaries of the soup societies of Philadelphia, circa 1862. The northeast corner shows the Kensington Soup Society's area. *Courtesy of John Connors.*

Moyamensing Soup Society: northwest corner of Eighth and Marriott Streets below Christian Street; lower side of Shippen (Bainbridge) Street, east of Broad Street.

Western Society, 1615 South Street: west side of Eleventh Street to Schuylkill River, south side of Race Street to north side of Shippen (Bainbridge) Street and west of Broad Street all south of Shippen (Bainbridge) Street.

Southern Society for Supplying the Poor with Soup: Griscom Street (late Green's Court) above Pine and between Fourth and Fifth Streets; east side of Eleventh Street to Delaware River, north side of Shippen (Bainbridge) Street to south side of Race Street.

Spring Garden Soup Society: Buttonwood Street below Broad Street; Sixth Street to Schuylkill River, north of Race Street.

Northern Soup Society: northeast corner of Fourth and Peter's Street above Brown Street; Sixth Street to Delaware River, north of Race Street.

Together the six societies also hammered out other issues like "bread no more than once a week" and the fact that they could distribute to "outsiders" but were to notify the "home" soup society of the occurrence so that a record was kept to prevent "double dipping." The coalition created a committee of one delegate each, which would meet and rectify the best method to make soup and determine the quality of bread for distribution.

Besides boundary determinations by this association of soup societies' meeting, there was also a meeting that year in order to "standardize the making of soup." A historian for Spring Garden Soup Society saw this effort as "doomed" from the start due to various factors, such as:

> *Each soup house had difficulty in getting supplies of meat and vegetables and often had to take what was available from their source of supply, even though it differed from the standard ingredients. Potatoes were basic ingredients. Other vegetables were seasonal and not available at all times. Refrigeration was dependent on ice and there was very little around except in winter.*

Also, the soup houses were competitive and did not always get along. "Jealousy and bad feeling between different organizations" appear to have been the norm. Much like today, where competing social service agencies vie for clients, the various soup societies fought over the boundaries they would serve; they eventually drew up a boundary map in 1862.

The Kensington Soup Society did not participate in those early meetings in 1857. Kensington was founded later than a number of these earlier societies and had only recently been incorporated in April 1853. The year after the incorporation of the Kensington Soup Society, Philadelphia County was consolidated into the city of Philadelphia, but Kensington was still considered outside of the core center of the city, where most of the old Soup Societies operated, for several years. However, by 1860 Kensington began to be listed in the Philadelphia city directories and sent delegates to the citywide coalition of soup societies.

On February 3, 1862, the *NA and U.S. Gazette* ran a short piece on the soup houses in the city, giving the corporate titles, the boundaries they served and the names authorized to receive contributions to their funds. It was mentioned that applicants to the soup societies were to "bear with them the recommendation of a responsible party, and if found worthy, will be furnished regularly with nourishment for themselves and families." The Kensington Soup Society boundaries were stated to be "From Laurel to Norris St., river Delaware to Front Street." These boundaries conform directly to what would have been called East Kensington at that time.

A committee of the various soup societies of Philadelphia, composed of one delegate from each, met on January 27, 1862. A member of the Western Soup Society proposed that three delegates from each soup society were to represent their respective society at an annual meeting of soup society organizations. The annual meeting would be held on the third Monday of each December. If there were not three delegates appointed by the respective soup societies, then the president, treasurer and secretary of the society would be the delegates. The proposal was accepted by all present.

This new coalition of citywide soup societies would also make itself available to meet at other times if needed. The purpose of this coalition was to "confer together, impart information, compare experiences, and endeavor to arrive at such conclusions as may tend to advance interests of perspective societies." Another main objective of the coalition was to set boundaries for each soup society regarding their service districts.

If we take a look at how the Southwark Soup Society conducted its society in the 1860s and compare it to the Kensington Soup Society as it was run

Philadelphia, December 12, 1863.

The Annual Meeting of the Joint Board of the Soup Societies of Philadelphia will be held on Tuesday evening next, 15th inst. at 7½ o'clock, at No. 800 Arch street, over the drug store. Will you be kind enough to notify the representatives of your Society of this meeting, and request their attendance?

Very Respectfully,

JOSEPH J. WILLIAMS,

Secretary of Joint Board,
1429 Arch Street.

To *Char M. Lukens Esq.* of *Kensington Soup Society.*

Invitation to Charles M. Lukens, requesting a representative for the annual meeting of the Joint Board of the Soup Societies of Philadelphia, December 12, 1863. *Kensington Soup Society Archives.*

in the 1870s, we can deduce the method chosen by Kensington for running its society.

The Southwark Soup Society in the 1860s appears to have had a fairly sophisticated operation, with standing committees composed of the following: property, legacies and trusts, auditing, finance, investigating, printing, supplies, distribution, collections, bread and fuel. The Collections Committee was particularly large, comprising twenty-one members. If you compare Southwark Soup Society with the Kensington Soup Society organization of the same time period, it would appear that the members delegated much of the actual work to the officers of the society.

The Kensington Soup Society had only a couple standing committees: the Soup House Committee and the Real Estate Committee. Other committees would be formed ad hoc and apparently disbanded once the objective of the committee had been attained. Kensington had one trustworthy individual hired as the collector, responsible for the solicitation and collection of funds. The collector was the "official agent" of the society. The steward was another trusted person of the Kensington Soup Society who was paid to visit and investigate potential clients. The four officers of the society would collect monies as well.

The duties of most of the Southwark Committees (legacies and trusts, auditing, finance and printing) were handled by the Kensington Soup Society's Board of Managers and officers at their regular meetings, or by their respective office. For example, the treasurer took care of all financial matters. Kensington's Soup House Committee took care of supplies, distribution, bread, etc. Things were more simplified at the Kensington Soup House, compared to the more bureaucratic structure of Southwark, which placed a greater emphasis on committee organization and had many more individuals involved.

CHAPTER 3

EARLY HOMES OF THE KENSINGTON SOUP SOCIETY AND THE FINANCING OF THE CREASE STREET SOUP HOUSE

EARLY HOMES OF THE SOUP SOCIETY— 208 AND 247 ALLEN STREET

The first location for the Kensington Soup Society at its founding in 1844 was allegedly 208 Allen Street. This site was located at the corner of Allen Street and Brusstar's Court, slightly north of Shackamaxon Street. Brusstar's, or Brewster's, Court was later called Stoy Avenue, and then in 1898 was renamed Day Street. Today this part of Day Street has long been obliterated.

Due to the smallness of the 208 Allen Street Soup House, the officers and managers would often have their annual meeting at the Kensington Methodist Episcopal Church (also known as "Old Brick Church"), as is evidenced in several election notices in the *Philadelphia Inquirer* and in the *North American & United States Gazette*, dated between December 30, 1859, and January 2, 1863.

While the actual address of the Soup House was 208 Allen Street, the 1860 Philadelphia city directory, the first directory in which the Kensington Soup Society appears, lists the Soup House at "Shackamaxon Street." Since Shackamaxon Street was more well known than Allen Street or Brusstar's Court, it was perhaps listed as such to better help direct people to the location.

The Soup Society was again advertised at "Shackamaxon Street" in the 1861 Philadelphia city directory, but in 1862 the address was finally given

The parking lot of the Edward Corner building, showing where 208 Allen Street once stood; this was the first home of the Kensington Soup Society. *Kensington Soup Society Archives.*

The second home of the Soup Society was at 247 Allen Street, just below Marlborough. The society was at this location from 1864 to 1870.

more correctly as 208 Allen Street. The city directories for the years 1863 through 1867 all list the Soup Society at this 208 Allen Street address, even though other evidence supports that the society moved the location of the Soup House to 247 Allen Street by at least January 1864.

There are a couple of occasions in January 1861 where it is advertised in the *Philadelphia Inquirer* that the Kensington Soup Society's Soup House is located at 208 Allen Street, and again it is advertised as such on a February 10, 1862 notice in the same newspaper. However, a *Philadelphia Inquirer* notice of January 12, 1864, states that the Kensington Soup House was on Allen Street, above Marlborough, which would seem to indicate that the society had moved to another location, presumably the 247 Allen Street address.

In the *Philadelphia Inquirer* again, this time on December 28, 1865, it states that the society will be holding its Annual Contributors Meeting at the Soup House at 247 Allen Street, below Marlborough, to elect the Board of Managers and officers. The Allen Street address being "below" and "above" is a bit confusing, but it would appear that both refer to the 247 Allen Street address. The Annual Contributors Meeting was held in 1865 at the Soup House on Allen Street and not at the Kensington ME "Old Brick" Church, which is another indication that the Soup House had moved from the smaller 208 Allen Street location to the larger space at 247 Allen.

A few months later, on February 26, 1866, the *Philadelphia Inquirer* reports that the Kensington Soup Society has been distributing soup from 247 Allen Street, near Marlborough, "for the past 45 days." Finally, another notice on January 28, 1867, also shows the Soup Society as located at 247 Allen Street. It would appear, then, that the Soup House was at 247 Allen Street for the 1866–67 season as well. These four articles from the *Philadelphia Inquirer* all seem to indicate that the Soup Society moved from 208 Allen Street to 247 Allen Street by at least January 1864, and possibly earlier, for the start of the 1863–64 season.

The Philadelphia city directory eventually lists the Kensington Soup Society at 247 Allen Street in the 1869 directory, so the earlier entries for 1865 through 1868 were probably erroneous. The 1864 directory would have been compiled in late 1863. It is probable that a careless compiler repeated the same address rather than check with the society. At the same time, one would think that the society would have notified the directory's publisher to correct its address as well, particularly after seeing the directory published incorrectly in 1865.

These newspaper notices and city directories of the 1860s indicate that the Kensington Soup Society was located at the 208 Allen Street address from at least January 1861 to February 1862, before moving to 247 Allen Street sometime between February 10, 1862, and January 1864. Most likely, the Soup Society was still at the 208 Allen Street address later than February 10, 1862, and the evidence that has been uncovered thus far supports this time frame. While tradition states that the society was at 208 Allen Street prior to 1861, there is no formal record to support it, except for the 1860 city directory that states its general address as Shackamaxon Street.

The Soup Society's place at 208 Allen was eventually found to be inadequate for the operations of the organization as the demand for soup increased in the neighborhood. The society reconnoitered and secured a larger place at 247 Allen Street, near Marlborough Street, where it remained until it secured the funds to purchase its own property and erect the present Soup House at 1036 Crease Street, where it still stands.

On January 1, 1870, the Kensington Soup Society advertised the election results from a few days previous on December 28, 1869. This January 1 advertisement stated its address as 247 Allen Street. The next year, on November 30, 1871, the Soup Society advertised an election from its Soup House at 1036 Crease Street. On January 3, 1871, the *Philadelphia Inquirer* announced that the Kensington Soup House at 1036 Crease Street would be open for the distribution of soup on Tuesday morning, January 3, 1871.

It would appear then that the Soup Society moved into the Crease Street property sometime between July 7, 1870, when it purchased the property, and November 30, 1871, when it first listed this place as its abode.

The original deed for the present Soup House indicates that the Soup Society purchased the lot on Crease Street on July 7, 1870, for $1,000 from John Lemark and his wife Jane. Signing the deed for the Soup Society were Charles M. Lukens and Thomas M. Montgomery, both officers of the society. Lukens and Montgomery were in the conveyance business, so it was natural for them to handle the purchasing of the property. John Lemark was a Philadelphia morocco dresser who had acquired the property the previous March from Beauveau Borie, Borie's wife Pattie and Richard R. Neill. It would appear to have been a simple investment opportunity for Lemark, as he sold it within four months of acquiring it.

The Crease Street property measured 25 feet on Crease Street with a depth of roughly 125 feet. It was located on the western side of Crease, 25 feet from the south side of Wildey Street. The Kensington Soup Society building on Crease Street was built by the society as a soup house, which allowed the members to run a more efficient operation as well as expand their capacity to distribute soup to the neighborhood residents.

Early Homes of the Kensington Soup Society and the Financing of the Crease Street Soup House

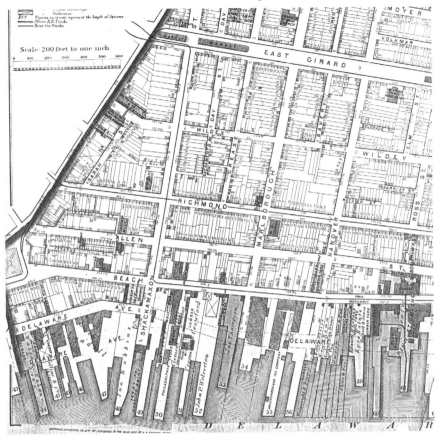

Hopkins 1876 map of Kensington showing the first, second and final locations of the Soup House: 208 and 247 Allen Street, and 1036 Crease Street.

Proposals for Expanding 247 Allen Street Soup House

The need for building a new soup house became evident in the early 1860s. The society was approaching its twentieth anniversary, and its work and the needs of the people of Kensington continued to expand. The Civil War brought more hardship to Kensington as mothers and children were without husbands and fathers for extended periods of time. When the men finally came home, some of them were lame or sick, and still others never returned at all.

During the Civil War, the Kensington Soup Society tried to expand its services by moving its operations from its original location at 208 Allen Street to 247 Allen Street. This move took place sometime between February 1862 and January 1864, and within a few years at this new location, the society was already beginning to plan for further expansion.

A committee was formed in early 1868 to "enquire into the expediency & feasibility of building a new Soup House, adjoining the Present one." The committee's report of January 30, 1868, shows that the Soup Society was already soliciting bids on the cost of building an adjacent soup house to the one currently in operation at 247 Allen Street. The 247 Allen Street Soup House was found to be the smallest in the city in its capacity to make soup, as well as the smallest in its ability to accommodate those needing the charity. The committee looking into the building of a new soup house consisted of William W. Taxis, John Robbins, George W. Vaughan, Charles M. Lukens and Alexander H. McFadden.

The committee report stated that Kensington had two 70-gallon kettles capable of making 140 gallons of soup, and its soup house could accommodate only 40 persons. These statistics made it the smallest in the city. The next smallest was the Central Soup Society, which was using two 90-gallon kettles, making 180 gallons of soup, with an ability to accommodate up to 70 people. The largest soup house was the Northern Soup Society, which had three 100-gallon kettles, furnishing 450 gallons of soup and a building that could accommodate 170 people. The Northern Soup Society was more than four times larger than Kensington in both production of soup and capacity to accommodate the people who showed up for soup. The Western Soup Society's building could accommodate the largest amount, up to 250, with a capacity of cooking 400 gallons of soup in its four 100-gallon kettles. Moyamensing Soup Society was able to cook only 180 gallons of soup in its two 90-kettles, but its facility held 150 people, almost four times as many as Kensington.

The committee reported that it gave out 279 tickets for soup but could only shelter 40 people, with the number of people daily increasing. The report went on to state:

> So you can form some idea of the large number of little ones, that are compelled to stand, outside of our doors, in all kinds of weather, and not only so, but we have a large number of adults, many of whom are females, who through poverty are obliged to accept of our charities, and we think it is an unjust infliction, to subject them to such crowding & inconveniences as necessarily occurs at our Soup House every day.
>
> We therefore gentlemen, in view of the above, would report that in our judgment it is both expedient & feasible to build a new Soup House and

Early Homes of the Kensington Soup Society and the Financing of the Crease Street Soup House

respectfully submit for your consideration and adoption, the accompanying plan & estimate.

There were a number of bidders who submitted plans and estimates to the Soup Society's committee. One, the most detailed, was from Christoph Steube; the other bidder was Wildey & Gardy, a local contractor. The bids were to build the Soup Society a one-story addition in the lot adjoining the north side of the 247 Allen Street Soup House, number 249–251 Allen Street. The building was to have a 31½-foot front on Allen Street, with a depth of 28½ feet, next to the "present soup house."

Steube proposed that he would remove the two kettles from the old Soup House, along with their foundations, expanding the old foundations and altering the fabric to make the place back into a dwelling. He would add a third kettle to the two older ones in the new building, installing all three with new foundations, as well as adding eleven burners. The new building was to have a full basement as well; the outdoor cellar entrance of the old building would be eliminated and access to the basement in that building would be made from inside the first floor.

The old Soup House building would be fixed up and rented out as a dwelling; only the walls would need to be rearranged. The new place would also have a small office. This larger building would provide a larger facility to accommodate the people, as well as expand the soup production by another seventy gallons, which would place Kensington in the middle of production and accommodations amongst the city's soup societies, just ahead of the Central and Moyamensing but still far behind the Western and Northern Soup Societies.

Steube's estimate of $1,947 was about $1,000 cheaper then Wildey & Gardy, and presumably he would have been in line for getting the contract. The plan for a new soup house got to the point where John Alley, a Marlborough Street neighbor whose property adjoined the Allen Street Soup House, agreed to "vacate as much of my yard as the Soup House Society may require to build a new Soup House & make yard for Mrs. Roberts." Alley was probably a tenant in a property he rented from the Soup Society.

While it appears that Steube would have come in as the low bidder, Jacob Jones, a member of the Board of Managers, also appears to have put in a bid, the contract of which reads identical to those of Christoph Steube and Wildey & Gardy. Jones's bid is dated March 1868, and a letter from committee member William W. Taxis to Charles M. Lukens instructs Lukens to "cut off the signature of Wildey & Gardy's estimate, and send the same to Jacob Jones, 423 Richmond Street, as a guide to him, in the construction of the Soup House, as he failed to take a copy of the bid he sent in." The letter is dated April 10, 1868. It could be that the committee wanted to make sure that the same work was being bid on by all parties, or perhaps Taxis was steering the contract to a fellow Board of Managers member.

The Soup Society's committee, formed to investigate a new soup house, reported back again to the Board of Managers in February 1868, stating that their investigations found that another proposal would not be feasible. That proposal called for the Soup Society to demolish houses it owned on Marlborough Street and build a three-story soup house that would also have bathing facilities. This proposal would cost $9,000, but the Soup Society only had $1,300 on hand. Its 247 Allen Street property would only be able to be sold for about $2,200, providing the society with a total of $3,500. The Board of Managers did not think it wise to go into debt for $5,500, as they also would lose the rental income from the demolished or sold Marlborough Street and Allen Street properties.

A third proposal before the committee was simply to expand the north side of the 247 Allen Street house, which would only cost about $1,500 but would not be big enough for what was needed. The Steube and the Wildey & Gardy plans seemed to be the best options for the Soup Society, and the committee recommended this option.

While it is unclear if this one-story addition on the north side of the 247 Allen Street Soup House ever came to fruition, it did get the Board of Managers to consider the idea of expanding the Soup House. It's hard to imagine the Soup House would expend several thousand dollars from its limited budget in 1868, only to turn around two years later in 1870 and purchase the Crease Street property and begin the process of building another Soup House. It would appear, unless other evidence is uncovered, that the expansion was delayed until July 1870, when the Soup Society finally purchased the 1036 Crease Street property and built its Soup House.

The plans to demolish the Marlborough Street houses that the society owned, as well as demolish the 247 Allen Street house that it owned, was opposed by some on the board due to the fact that the properties supplied rental income to the Soup Society. Thus, this idea was not put into effect. While serving as the Soup House, the 247 Allen Street property also brought in some rental income, as is evidenced by an agreement dated

Early Homes of the Kensington Soup Society and the Financing of the Crease Street Soup House

March 23, 1867, in which Eliza Brooks agreed to pay the Kensington Soup Society sixty dollars annually for the rent of the 247 Allen Street property starting April 1 of that year. However, she was to leave the second story of the property "reserved for the exclusive use of the Managers of the Kensington Soup Society and also that such part of the House as may be needed during the months of December, January, February & March for the making and distribution of Soup shall be likewise reserved for the Society." It would appear that the Soup Society rented the property out during off season and allowed Brooks to live on the first and third floors during the soup season, thus decreasing her rent (perhaps by thirty or more dollars per year), which would normally have been a bit more. Brooks was also asked in the agreement "to keep the house in good condition."

ALEXANDER H. MCFADDEN'S FINANCING OF THE CREASE STREET SOUP HOUSE

The financing and construction of the 1036 Crease Street Soup House appears to have been accomplished with the help of one of the society's Board of Managers, Alexander H. McFadden. McFadden was on the original committee of 1868 that looked into building a new Soup House. He lived locally at 1029 Shackamaxon Street and became a member of the Board of Managers during the season of 1862. He became the vice-president of the Soup Society in 1880 and held that position until he was elected the president in 1883 upon the death of George J. Hamilton. He remained president until his own death in May 1900. In all, he had a thirty-eight-year commitment to the Soup Society. McFadden served on the House Committee for at least the years 1873 to 1883, resigning from the committee when he became president. He also served on several other committees: Property (1875–76), Entertainment (1878–79), Bath House (1879–80), Real Estate (1882–83) and Church Collections (1884–85).

McFadden made his money in the iron business with the firm of McFadden, Gaulbert & Caskey, located at American and York Streets. When he died, he was considered the oldest ironmaster in the city. He was born in Cecil County, Maryland, on April 28, 1820. In Maryland, he learned the millwright trade and was very successful, building many mills all over that state. He moved to Philadelphia in 1856 and began the manufacture of sheet metal with the firm of Marshall, Philips, & Co., at that time located on Kensington's Marlborough Street wharf. He closed his partnership with

A.H. McFadden, iron monger, served on the Soup Society's board for thirty-eight years (1862–1900) and as its president for the last seventeen years of his life.

this firm in 1877 and became a partner in the Fairhill Rolling Mills, which later became the firm of McFadden, Gaulbert & Caskey, where he remained until he died.

McFadden was always active in charitable work. Besides the Kensington Soup Society, he was one of the oldest members of Kensington ME "Old Brick" Church, president of the Penn Widows Asylum and a manager of the Methodist Episcopal Hospital. He was also a director of Dickinson College at Carlisle, Pennsylvania, and a director of the Northern National Bank.

Alexander H. McFadden would also appear to have advanced the money for either the purchase and/or building of the Crease Street Soup House, as there are a number of receipts from McFadden in which the secretary of the Soup Society, George J. Hamilton, was making regular payments to McFadden with interest on a mortgage that McFadden held against the real estate of the Soup Society.

In October 1871, Hamilton paid McFadden $108 for six months' interest on a mortgage of $3,600, paying eight days late. In November 1874, Hamilton paid McFadden $60 in full of interest on mortgage. This payment

Early Homes of the Kensington Soup Society and the Financing of the Crease Street Soup House

A 1950s-era photograph showing the 1036 Crease Street Soup House from a side view, showing garages along Crease and Wildey Streets. *Kensington Soup Society Archives.*

was also paid late by a month and ten days. The payment of $60 is lower than the 1871 payment of $108, which would seem to indicate that the loan was being paid down. Six months later, in June and August 1875, Hamilton paid McFadden another $60 for six months' interest that was for a stated mortgage that still had $2,000 due. Between October 1871 and June–August 1875, the Soup Society appears to have paid back McFadden $1,600 on the loan, as well as interest. Later in 1875, in November, and again in April 1876, Hamilton made two payments to McFadden for $60 each for the two six months' interest on the $2,000 mortgage. In March 1877, the Soup Society still had the $2,000 mortgage due, but was able to pay the $60 on the six months' interest, actually paying a couple of days in advance. In December 1877, the six-month payments decreased to $54 every six months, presumably because the society had paid off some of the principal. Finally, in January 1880, the Soup Society was able to pay McFadden $400 on the principal of the mortgage on the 1036 Crease Street property, and again in April of the same year, another $400 was paid to McFadden. By March 1882, McFadden was paid $500 by the Soup Society against the note he held on the real estate of the Soup House. These flurries of payments to the principal ($1,300 between 1880 and 1882) might mean that the loan was coming due, or it could also mean that the Soup Society, with McFadden now being the vice-president of the society, did not want any conflict of interest and wanted to pay him off in a hurry.

In addition to this mortgage on the Soup Society's real estate, evidence exists in the society's files that shows the firm of Pancoast & Maule (composed of the partnership of Henry B. Pancoast and Francis I. Maule) held a note written by McFadden for the Soup Society in 1871, before McFadden was an officer of the society. It would appear that Pancoast & Maule must have either installed or provided the material for the steam and water heating systems in the new Soup House on Crease Street and that McFadden paid for the work and material. There is a receipt for a note of A.H. McFadden for $694 owed to Pancoast & Maule, where McFadden carried the note for the Soup Society. McFadden would appear to have written a note on January 17, 1871, that was payable in sixty days. It is unclear if the $3,600 mortgage that McFadden had against the Soup House included this $694 due to Pancoast & Maule. Pancoast & Maule were iron merchants and presumably McFadden would have known them through his own involvement in the iron trade.

The deed for the purchase of the 1036 Crease Street property shows that the Soup Society bought the property for $1,000. Records of the society show that McFadden was due $3,600 by the Soup Society. Further records show Pancoast & Maule had a note against McFadden for the Soup House. Combined, this evidence would appear to conclude that Alexander H. McFadden helped with the purchase, financing and construction of the Soup House on Crease Street.

On August 27, 1870, David Dickerson, chairman of the Building Committee, requested in a letter to Soup Society treasurer George J. Hamilton that he pay Philadelphia architect Thomas S. Levy $3,000 as the first payment toward the erection of the new Soup House on Crease Street.

CHAPTER 4

THE RUNNING OF THE SOUP SOCIETY

THE ANNUAL CONTRIBUTORS MEETING

The Kensington Soup Society's Annual Contributors Meetings were generally held once a year on the first Thursday of November or December. At these meetings, only individuals who contributed to the support of the Soup Society would be eligible to nominate and elect individuals to the Board of Managers. The right to vote was limited to those who had paid their subscription. The subscription rate in the nineteenth century was two dollars per year.

Once the panel of nominations was announced, voting would take place. A judge and two tellers would be appointed, usually from the managers of the preceding year's board. After the vote, the new Board of Managers was announced, the Annual Contributors Meeting adjourned, the new Board of Managers was organized and a meeting of the new Board of Managers was held.

THE BOARD OF MANAGERS

Once the new Board of Managers was organized, its members would immediately meet to nominate and elect officers for the upcoming season. In the nineteenth century, five members were needed to hold a quorum and conduct business. The officer positions up for election were president, vice-president, treasurer and secretary. There was rarely a change in the officer positions unless there was a death or geographical relocation of an officer due to retirement or illness.

PRESIDENT

An unknown portrait of one of the Soup Society's presidents, possibly Abraham P. Eyre, George Stockham, Honorable John Robbins or Edward W. Gorgas. *Kensington Soup Society Archives.*

During the nineteenth century the following gentlemen held the position of president of the Kensington Soup Society:

Abraham P. Eyre, 1854–62
George Stockham, 1862–72
Honorable John Robbins, 1872–80
Edward W. Gorgas, 1880–82
George J. Hamilton, 1882–83
Alexander H. McFadden, 1883–99

The president of the society was responsible for presiding at all meetings of the board to maintain order, sign all orders of the treasurer and call special meetings if needed (at the written request of three members of the board).

It was also the president's responsibility to appoint such committees as the board might direct.

VICE-PRESIDENT

The vice-presidents of the Kensington Soup Society during the nineteenth century were as follows:

Eli Garrison Sr., 1854–70
Edward W. Gorgas, 1871–80
Alexander H. McFadden, 1880–83
Joseph Lippincott, 1883–97
Jacob Jones, 1897–99

Edward W. Gorgas, founder, manager and president of the Soup Society, also sold wood to the Soup Society, as shown here in 1879. *Kensington Soup Society Archives.*

The vice-president was to preside at all meetings of the board in the absence of the president, and in the case of death or resignation, he was to act as president until another election was held. If the president and vice-president were both absent from a meeting, then a "chairman pro tem" was to be appointed by the managers' meeting so that business could proceed.

SECRETARY

The secretary's office had the least turnover in the nineteenth century, due to the longevity of Charles M. Lukens's term. Only two men held the office of secretary during this time:

Jacob K. Vaughan, 1854–61
Charles M. Lukens, 1861–99

The secretary of the society was in charge of the financial records and papers of the society. He was also the officer responsible for notifying all members of the board of meetings, giving public notice of the annual election and keeping correct minutes of the proceedings of all the meetings of the board in a book provided by the society. In the discontinuance of his position, the secretary was to make sure that his books and papers were handed over to his successor. Another responsibility of the secretary was to countersign all orders on the request of the treasurer when bills needed to be paid. Since there are no minutes of the society for the years prior to 1875, we can assume that some secretary along the way did not fulfill his duties and hand over the ledgers to his successor.

TREASURER

The treasurer's position also did not see much turnover, as George J. Hamilton and George Kessler held the post for most of the nineteenth century. William W. Taxis also held the treasurer's position during this period. The years that these three men held this position were as follows:

George J. Hamilton, 1854–82
William W. Taxis, 1882–84
George Kessler, 1884–99

The treasurer of the society received and held all moneys collected for or belonging to the society. The treasurer was to pay all orders signed by the president and secretary, and to keep an accurate account of all receipts and expenditures. The treasurer was required to report at each meeting of the board the state and condition of the treasury. The treasurer's books were to be open for the inspection of any member of the board or a committee appointed for examination, and in case of discontinuance in office, his books, papers and the funds belonging to the society were to be handed over to his successor.

Besides the elected positions of the Board of Managers, there were also several appointed and paid positions: collector, visitor and steward.

Top: George J. Hamilton (1801–1883) was a treasurer of the Soup Society. His mother's uncle was William Ball, heir to the Ball Estate, or Port Richmond.
Middle: Henry Kessler, brother to George Kessler, served thirty-eight years on the board of the Soup Society and helped to operate the Kessler Wagon Works.
Bottom: George Kessler was a thirty-two-year member of the Board of Managers of the Soup Society and founder of Kessler Wagon Works at Girard Avenue and Norris Street.

THE COLLECTOR

Daniel B. Mickle, 1861–62
John G. Hopkins, 1862–65
John C. Clouds, 1865–66
Daniel B. Mickle, 1866–71
David Dickerson, 1871–99

After the election and organization of the new Board of Managers for the upcoming year, the board would immediately appoint a collector whose responsibility was to collect monies for the society. Although anyone on the Board of Managers could accept donations to the Soup Society, the collector was the official agent for the society. This was a paid position, and remuneration included a certain percentage of the money raised. For the years 1875 to 1900, the commission was 8 percent of what the collector collected; for several years prior to that period (at least 1870–75) it was 10 percent. The collector also appeared to receive a commission on articles that were donated to the Soup Society. Apparently, the Board of Managers would estimate a monetary figure for the value of the donated articles (food, coal, etc.) and the collector would get the normal commission for those donations as if they were monetary donations.

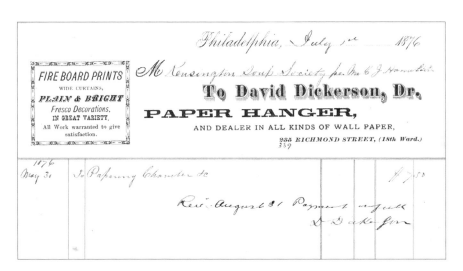

David Dickerson was a collector for the Soup Society for thirty-three years. He operated a paperhanging business, and this invoice shows him papering the Sugar House in 1876. *Kensington Soup Society Archives.*

One longtime collector was David Dickerson, formerly of 235 and later 339 Richmond Street. Dickerson was born in 1828 and by 1880 was already a widower. He was a one-time next-door neighbor to Oakley A. Cowdrick, who served on the Board of Managers for the Soup Society in the 1870s and 1880s. Cowdrick was also the first person appointed to the visitor position when the Soup Society created it in 1879.

Besides being a longtime collector for the Soup Society, Dickerson was also a longtime elected member of the Board of Managers. He served on the board from at least 1867 to 1906, a full thirty-nine years. Dickerson held the collector's position for at least thirty-three of those years, from 1871 until 1904.

Dickerson also served on a number of committees over the years: Committee on Conference with Richmond Soup Society, 1879–80; House Committee, 1879–80, 1884–1906; Committee on Bath House, 1879–80; Committee on Entertainment, 1882–83; and Committee for Appointing Steward, 1885–86.

Along with his work for the Soup Society, Dickerson also had a wallpapering business with his brother William and occasionally he is mentioned in the society's minutes as being paid for wallpapering work done at the Soup House.

The commissions collected for the position of collector were good, and one can see why Dickerson kept the position for all those years. In an average year during the 1870s, one could earn from $100 to $125 in commissions. The available receipts that have been preserved by the Soup Society show the money collected by Mickle and Dickerson and the commissions they kept. Table 2 below shows the ten-year period of 1870 to 1879. While the records are not complete for this decade, the available records do provide us with a glimpse of the amount of money involved:

TABLE 2: Money collected between 1870 and 1879 by the Soup Society's collectors and the commissions that were paid to them.

Year	Collected	Commission	% Commission
1870	$1,141.50	$114.15	10%
1871	$1,111.50	$111.15	10%
1872	$380.80	$38.08	10%
1873	$1,215.60	$121.56	10%

The Running of the Soup Society

1874	$1,048.00	$104.80	10%
1875	$1,240.00	$124.00	10%
1876	$1,207.13	$105.61	8%–10%*
1877	$1,119.18	$89.58	8%
1878	$144.75	$11.58	8%
1879	$1,559.00	$124.76	8%

*Commission appears to have started at 10 percent but then was decreased to 8 percent. In a meeting dated March 30, 1876, the subject was first brought up by Henry Kessler, who proposed the collector's commission to be cut in half to 5 percent. It was tabled over to the beginning of the next season after the annual elections. At a meeting of December 7, 1876, the price for the collector's commissions was reduced from 10 to 8 percent.

While for some years the collections were low (1872 and 1878), these figures do not represent the totals collected, but only the receipts that were preserved. The annual collections by the collector were more in line with the figures for other years. For the season of 1876–77, the receipts that have been preserved just about match the amounts noted in the meeting minute ledgers for that year.

THE VISITOR

Oakley A. Cowdrick, 1879–84
William C. Mohler, 1884–88
Charles C. McCormick, 1888–93
William C. Mohler, 1893–99

The Soup Society's visitor position was an appointed office that was created by the Board of Managers at its first meeting of the season. The position was created in January 1879 as a way to make sure that each soup applicant was indeed "worthy" of the society's charity and also that the applicant actually lived within the Soup Society's boundaries.

During the first month of the creation of this position (January 1879), the visitor called on close to five hundred applicants. The visitor position was a paid position, receiving ten cents per visit, which was later raised to fifteen cents per visit in 1893. After the initial start-up phase of this position, where upward of five hundred visits were needed to weed out the non-deserving, the number of people who actually had to be visited every month was not that great.

The position of visitor came about in January 1879 when the Committee of Five—the committee created to oversee the interests of the society as it pertained to protective measures of distributing soup—reported on the "bummers," those men who "have no fixed home or residence and [were] not men of families[,] but who go about gathering up something to eat wherever they can get it [and] who by the course of their lives are scarcely deserving of the Soup given them."

As a way to protect itself from these bummers, the committee presented a resolution that would create the position of visitor, an employed position of the society who "shall be present every morning at the office and receive the names of such applicants as the Committee may submit for inquiry and report next morning...said visitor shall be subject to the direction of the House Committee and continue so long in the service of the Society as the Committee may think advisable for the interest of the Society." The visitor was to call on all of the applicants in question at their stated residences to see if they indeed lived in the boundaries of the society and were deserving of aid.

At this meeting in January 1879, the resolution was accepted and the position of visitor was created. Oakley A. Cowdrick, already a member of the Board of Managers, became the first visitor in 1879 and held the position until 1884, when it was taken over by fellow board member William C. Mohler. Mohler kept the position for several years before yielding it to Charles C. McCormick. McCormick had taken over the job of steward at the Soup House after John and Mary Frazier had vacated the place. McCormick, who was not on the Board of Managers, held both the steward position from 1886 to 1897 and the visitor position from 1888 to 1893, when it perhaps became too difficult for him to make his visits and also help run the Soup House. More likely, he decided that the payment of ten cents per visit was not worth the effort.

After McCormick quit the visitor job in 1893, the Board of Managers increased the salary for the visitor position from ten to fifteen cents per visit, perhaps as an incentive to secure a new person to take over the position vacated by McCormick. William C. Mohler, who had previously held the position but had given it up to McCormick, took over the visitor position again in 1893 and held it until the end of the decade (1899).

In the first report of the newly created position of visitor (January 16, 1879), Oakley A. Cowdrick stated that he visited 228 applicants' homes,

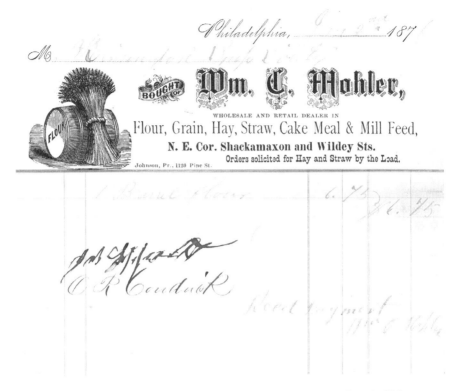

William C. Mohler was one of several merchants on the Soup Society's Board of Managers who made money by selling goods to the society. *Kensington Soup Society Archives*.

with 50 of them, or a little over 20 percent of the applicants, being rejected. Cowdrick's next report of January 23, 1879, saw 58 of 256 applicants being rejected, which again amounted to over 20 percent of the applicants. The weeding out of bummers and non-local applicants had begun.

At a meeting in January 1879, one of the directors, Samuel M. McCutcheon, thought that bummers in the "future be required to pay five cents per bowl of soup," at which the more humanitarian A.H. McFadden countered that if they did not have any money, they should still be furnished with soup. It seemed that some on the board of directors were not so keen about being so stringent with the poor, whether they were bummers or not. The motion was moved to the House Committee with power to act, in particular to act on those not living within the society's boundaries. This issue remained dormant for a couple of years, until it was brought up again in a meeting of the Board of Managers on December 14, 1882, where it was decided to "dispense with feeding bummers" altogether.

In another report by O.A. Cowdrick, this time on February 13, 1879, he stated that 16 out of 32 applicants he visited were rejected, and an additional report of February 27, 1879, showed only 2 of 15 families being rejected. For the part of the season (January–March 1879) when the visitor position was first created, 126 of the 531 homes visited were rejected, or just a little over 23 percent. Cowdrick's first report for the new season of 1879–80, which started in December 1879, shows that only 1 of the 58 homes he visited was rejected. Clearly the idea of the visitor had caught on and the "double dippers" and "undeserving" were now going elsewhere to try and get their charity. Apparently, after the initial mass visiting (almost 500 households in January 1879 alone), the number of homes that needed to be visited had decreased and most of the bummers and non-locals had been dispensed with.

Surviving records also show that while Cowdrick was visitor, he was also the officer responsible on the House Committee for "special cases." He would write letters of recommendation for families or individuals in order to be eligible for groceries. The family or individual would take Cowdrick's note to a local grocer, someone like W.H. Heiss & Bros., at Front and Girard, and could redeem the note for the amount written. In general it was usually one or two dollars' worth of groceries.

STEWARD/STEWARDESS (SUPERINTENDENT)

Jane Roberts, 1860–70
Robert Frazier, 1871–85
Mrs. Mary Frazier, 1885–86
Charles C. McCormick, 1886–97
Jeremiah Lyshon, 1897–99

At the first meeting of the newly elected Board of Managers, a steward, sometimes called the superintendent, would generally be appointed. The steward's position was a paid position and it did not need to be filled by a member of the Board of Managers. The salary for the steward position appears to have been $10.00 a week when Jane Roberts was steward in the 1860s. When Robert Frazier took over the post by at least January 1871, the salary was raised to $12.00 a week. Frazier got a raise to $14.00 a week by the following year in January 1872, and then another raise to $16.50 a week by February 1873. He held the position for at least the years 1871 to 1885 and his salary remained stable at $16.50. When he left the position in 1885, the job continued to be paid the same amount through at least the end of the century.

A woman by the name of Jane Roberts appears to have been the steward for at least the period from 1860 to 1870. She might have actually been the steward earlier than 1860, but without records it is hard to determine. Six receipts exist for the period from January to March 1870 that show her salary was ten dollars per week "for services at Soup House."

In the 1861 Philadelphia city directory, we find a Jane Roberts, the widow of Charles C. Roberts, living at 208 Allen Street, the original address of the first Kensington Soup House. It appears that the Soup Society allowed Roberts to live and work at the Soup House, a tradition that followed with successive stewards.

Jane Roberts is found listed in the 1860 census for Philadelphia as a forty-five-year-old woman with five children. Her oldest child was a boy named Charles, the same given name as her late husband, whose name was found in the 1861 city directory. This would appear to be the same woman as the one listed at 208 Allen Street in 1861. Mrs. Roberts was enumerated in Kensington's eighteenth ward, listed as running a boardinghouse. Besides her children, she had four boarders living with her. Checking the 1861 city directory against the 1860 census, we find that Jane Roberts was indeed running a boardinghouse out of the 208 Allen Street Soup House building.

The census was taken in June 1860, at a time when the Soup House was closed. The Board of Managers presumably allowed Mrs. Roberts to run a boardinghouse during the months the Soup House was not being occupied, perhaps as a way for additional income for the Soup Society. Mrs. Roberts lived at the Soup House for a number of years, even moving with it when the Soup House relocated from 208 Allen Street to 247 Allen Street.

Jane Roberts's name shows up in minutes from a meeting of the Soup Society for February 7, 1867. At this meeting she is recorded as paying nine dollars in rent. In December 1867, February 1868 and February 1869, the Soup Society is found to be making payments to Roberts of six dollars, nine dollars and nine dollars, respectively, so she presumably was not only renting from the society but was also still working for it.

According to a note in the minutes of a Board of Managers meeting held February 11, 1869, Jane Roberts would be vacating the 247 Allen Street property. However, as late as March 1870, we still find a "J. Roberts" listed in the Soup Society accounts, paying rent for an unspecified property. Since the Soup Society purchased the Crease Street property in July 1870, Roberts would have been at one of the other previous Soup Houses, probably 247 Allen Street. She paid seventy-two dollars for eight months of rent (nine dollars per month), which was to end in November 1870, the payments starting back in March 1870.

Next to Jane Roberts on the list of March 1870 is "J. Alley," who is also recorded as paying rent. Alley was the tenant who was willing to vacate part of his yard to expand the 247 Allen Street Soup House in 1868. He lived on the corner of Marlborough and Allen Streets, next to the 247 Allen Street Soup House.

An early *Philadelphia Inquirer* article shows Robert Frazier as the superintendent in 1872, and the society's monthly meeting minutes ledger lists him as the steward until 1885. There is a receipt for his services as early as January 26, 1871. The titles of steward and superintendent were at times interchangeable.

For his salary, Frazier was expected to work at the Soup House during the hours of the months of operation, December through March, as well as take care of the basic maintenance of the Soup House. For larger maintenance jobs at the Soup House and general laboring work, Frazier could earn additional income by doing the work himself rather then parceling it out to contractors.

The steward could live at the Soup House and was expected to maintain the house as well as help with running the Soup House during the winter months of the soup season. When John Frazier was at the position (1871–85), he was recorded as paying $10.42 a month for living at the Soup House. His rent did not increase for almost fifteen years, nor was the rent raised when his wife took over the position or when Charles C. McCormick took the post. For the years 1871 to 1897, a full twenty-eight years, the rent on the Soup House for the steward stayed at $10.42 a month.

There were also times (April–September 1884) when the Board of Managers allowed Frazier to live rent free for six months, during the off-season of the Soup House. Presumably, Frazier would still have been responsible for caring for the building.

When John Frazier's wife, Mary, took over the steward duties, she too received the same pay, $16.50 a week, as her husband. Records also indicate that Mary was already receiving payments here and there "for services" at the Soup House before she took over the position from her husband.

Charles C. McCormick took over the steward position after only one year of Mary Frazier serving in that capacity. He also received $16.50 a week for

John Frank Fox served on the Board of Managers for twenty-five years. He had a wood and flour business at 463 East Girard Avenue.

his troubles. While the rent did not go up in twenty-eight years, neither did the salary for the position.

McCormick had taken over the job of steward at the Soup House after John and Mary Frazier vacated the place. McCormick, who was not a manager of the society, held both the steward (1886–97) and the visitor (1888–93) positions.

Jeremiah Lyshon took over the superintendent's job from McCormick and kept the post for eighteen years (1897–1915). His wages and rent remained the same until at least the end of the nineteenth century.

The Committees of the Soup Society

Unlike several soup societies that had many standing committees (such as the Southwark Soup Society, which had at least eleven standing committees), the Kensington Soup Society exhibited just a couple of standing committees and would generally depend on the officers and several staff persons to take care of much of the business of the society.

The Kensington Soup Society's House Committee, a regular standing committee, would generally form for the upcoming year at the first meeting of the year for the newly elected Board of Managers. The House Committee reported to the Board of Managers at every meeting. It was the committee's responsibility to report on the amount of charity given out in the preceding weeks. It would also recommend changes in distribution of the charity if needed. A typical House Committee report would give the details of how many pints of soup and loaves of bread (if any) were given out, as well as the number of families served. These accounts would also report on the number of actual individuals (adults and children) served and how many "wayfarers" showed up that past week. If there were other items that were given out, such as coal or vegetables, they would report on that as well.

The Real Estate Committee (in its early days called the Property Committee and later combined with the House Committee) was also a standing committee. This committee had the authority to make necessary repairs on the Soup House. The bills for these repairs were paid by the treasurer once the Real Estate Committee authorized him to act. The Real Estate Committee also would generally consider and oversee any real estate investment properties owned by the Soup House.

Besides these two standing committees, there would occasionally be other committees formed when issues arose, such as a special Boundaries Committee when it was necessary to formulate exact boundaries for the various soup societies to prevent double dipping by applicants, or an Entertainment Committee that was started to raise funds for the society's treasury.

THE SOUP HOUSE HOURS OF OPERATION

The Soup House was open every day except Sundays. The Board of Managers, at their meetings in December and March, determined the actual opening and closing dates of the Soup House for each season. In general, the Soup House was open for twelve weeks, from the middle of December through the middle of March.

The side entrance to the Soup House, with a sign showing it is open "Mon. thru Fri. 11 a.m. to 1 p.m, Nov to March."

Elections

The elections for the Soup Society for the last quarter of the nineteenth century (1875–1900) were rarely contested. A group of men would be ceremoniously nominated to the Board of Managers and they would all be elected unanimously.

In the complete meeting minutes of the Kensington Soup Society that are available for the nineteenth century (1875–99), there were only a couple of incidents when elections were contested. One of these contested elections took place on December 16, 1880, when for the first time in the written records of the society individuals nominated for the Board of Managers were not elected. Joseph S. Allen, Dr. Edward Down, Christopher B. Porter and John O. Hughes were all nominated but not elected. Whether this shows any signs of factions emerging is unclear. It might just be that the society was lucky enough to have so many people willing to volunteer to help with service. The Board of Managers had been set at twenty-five to twenty-six members for a number of years (since at least the annual report of 1873–74), so perhaps since there were thirty-one nominations in 1880, only the first twenty-six got the position.

Joseph S. Allen, one of those not chosen at this contested election, could possibly be the same individual who is listed on the Board of Managers in the society's annual report of 1873–74. That report showed a Joseph S. Allen as a manager. Dr. Edward Down would eventually be elected to the board for the years 1897–99, as would John O. Hughes for the years 1881–93. However, Christopher B. Porter seems to have been discouraged or moved away, as he never volunteered or was nominated again.

At the Annual Contributors Meeting of December 4, 1884, another contested election occurred. After the contributors elected a Board of Managers, the managers had their meeting to elect officers. For the position of treasurer, two individuals were nominated for the first time, George Kessler and J. Howard Marshall. The previous treasurer, W.W. Taxis, had recently died and left the position vacant. Kessler had been on the Board of Managers since 1875, whereas Marshall was a relative newcomer, having been on the board for only one year. After a ballot was taken, Kessler won the position of treasurer. If there was any animosity, it would have to be set aside, as both men were appointed by President McFadden to be on the House Committee that year. George Kessler would go on and serve as the society's treasurer for the rest of the century.

The Running of the Soup Society

In this same year, 1884, when the committees were formed at the next meeting, Oakley Cowdrick declined to serve as visitor and W.C. Mohler took over the position. Cowdrick eventually resigned as a manager of the Soup Society, and left the board after the 1884–85 season. Not enough research has been done to determine what happened to Cowdrick—was he simply too old, or was he retiring and moving away?

Besides these few contested elections, the Soup Society ran fairly smoothly, with no rivals for the quarter century for which complete meeting minute records are available.

CHAPTER 5

The Soup House in the Late Nineteenth Century

The Expansion Years of the Kensington Soup House

During the 1860s, the Kensington Soup Society expanded its soup distribution operations by moving from the original small soup house at 208 Allen Street to a slightly larger facility at nearby 247 Allen Street. Still later, in 1870, the Soup Society purchased the Crease Street property and built for the first time a building that was expressly designed as a soup house. These efforts to expand and meet the demands of the residents of Kensington came under the directorship of George Stockham, who served as the Soup Society's president for the decade from 1862 to 1872. With the expansion to 247 Allen Street and then to the greatly expanded Crease Street Soup House, the Kensington Soup Society was better able to meet the needs of Kensington's poor.

During the Civil War years (1860–65), when the charity of the Soup House was highly needed, the Soup Society, besides calling for monetary contributions, also called for contributions of flour, meat, vegetables and even wood. As early as 1861, the Soup House at 208 Allen Street was distributing 1,040 pints of soup a day, with bread. The demand was so great that the Soup Society was forced to advertise for contributions, as it was "not able to supply the demands of the needful, which are daily increasing."

A report published in the local paper in February 1866 stated that during a forty-two-day period in the 1865–66 season, the Soup House distributed

REMEMBER THE POOR.

The KENSINGTON SOUP SOCIETY are now distributing, daily, Soup and Bread, to about three hundred families, many of whom are in the most destitute condition: and, in order to carry on this work, they now appeal for aid from those sympathizing with these poor and needy creatures. They therefore ask of you a contribution of Two Dollars, which will constitute you an annual member of the Society.

Respectfully Yours,

GEORGE STOCKHAM, *Pres't,*
ELI GARRISON, *Vice Pres't,*
GEORGE J. HAMILTON, *Treas.,*
CHARLES M. LUKENS, *Sec.*

Any donations of Meat, Flour, or Vegetables, will be thankfully received.

DANIEL B. MICKLE, *Agent & Collector.*

Please retain this circular until called for.

"Remember the Poor," appeal notice, circa 1860s, asking for money to help support the "destitute condition" of the residents of Kensington. *Kensington Soup Society Archives.*

5,250 gallons of soup. It amounted to an average of 125 gallons per day, with upward of 2,500 loaves of bread given out three times a week. In all, the Soup Society fed 1,100 people each day that it was opened.

Even after the war, the letup did not come. Already set up in the new 247 Allen Street Soup House, in a one-week period during January 1867 the society gave out 3,240 pints of soup, along with 1,463 loaves of bread, to 287 families made up of 1,060 people. The call for help that went out stated, "The institution is cramped in its work for lack of means, and deserves a liberal patronage."

Since the Soup Society records are all but lost for the period prior to November 1875, we have to rely on the newspaper appeals and advertisements in order to see what the distribution numbers were for the Soup House. One report given right before the 1873–74 annual report (which was printed and still survives) was found in the *Philadelphia Inquirer* of December 12, 1872. This report stated that the Soup Society gave out 12,600 gallons of soup during the previous season (1870–71), averaging 140 gallons a day, with 75 pounds of meat per day being consumed. There were 100 bushels of potatoes and 15 barrels of beans used during that season. The income from all sources was $1,703.85, with general expenses being $1,675.43. The interest on the mortgage of the new Soup House on Crease Street was $216.00, and they had $400.00 invested to aid in the payment of the mortgage on the building. The final analysis was that the Kensington Soup Society was $3,600.00 in debt and "contributions are earnestly invited to meet the incubus."

CONTRIBUTORS FOR 1873-74.

"The Lord loveth a cheerful giver."

Adaire & Mullica $5 00	Cash, (Dolan) $5 00	Gorgas, E. W $2 00	McFadden, A. H. $2 00
Allen, Joseph S 2 00	Cobb & Sheets 5 00	Glass, Alexander 2 00	McBride, W. F 5 00
	Caldwell, J. E. & Co 5 00	Guyant, David 2 00	Middleton, C. W. & H. ... 5 00
Becker, H. & Co 5 00	Christian, Henry 5 00	Grove, Geo. W., Estate } 500 00	Martin, James & Co 5 00
Brady, W. H. & Co 5 00	Cumming, D. B. 5 00	by kindness of Ex'rs. }	McNelly, Edward 5 00
Bennett & Co 5 00	Cooper, Mr. (Donation)... 20 00	George, Jesse, Estate } 500 00	Mellor, Bains & Mellor... 5 00
Bradlee & Co 5 00	Cash, (a Friend) 2 00	by kindness of Ex'rs. }	Marshall, Bros. & Co...... 10 00
Baird, William M 5 00			Morris, J. P. & Co 10 00
Bacon, B. R. 2 00	Drexell & Co 20 00	Horner, A.. Jr 10 00	McKee, Jos. D 10 00
Barnard, James 2 00	Derbyshire, Alexander J. 10 00	Hood, Bonbright & Co..... 10 00	McKean, Newhall & Borie 10 00
Birely, Hillman &} 10 00	Day, George 10 00	Hodgson, J. B., & Neph'w 10 00	Morris, Tasker & Co 10 00
Streaker }	Dornen, Maybin & Co..... 5 00	Hughes & Patterson 5 00	Mason, James S. 5 00
Browning & Bros 10 00	Dougherty, J. A. & Sons.. 5 00	Heyl, Gibbons & Co 5 00	Michener, J. H. & Co...... 5 00
Bailey, Joel T. & Co...... 10 00	Dubois & Aitken 2 00	Harrison, Thomas 5 00	Malone, W & Sons 5 00
Borie, C. & H 10 00	Davis, John G. 5 00	Hemphill, Joseph 2 00	
Baeder, Adamson & Co... 10 00	Deily & Fowler 5 00	Hoff, Fontain & Abbott .. 5 00	Nyce, William 10 00
Brown, Bros. & Co. 10 00	Davis, James P. 5 00	Howell & Bros 5 00	Neafie & Levy 10 00
Brown & Woelpper 5 00	Davis, Capt. 5 00	Hamilton, Geo. J. 2 00	Norris, Isaac 20 00
Bruner & Davis 5 00	Day, Robert H. 2 00		N———, S— 5 00
Bunting.Durburrow & Co. 10 00	Dittie, James 2 00	Irwin & Stinson 10 00	Norris, Henry 5 00
Butterworth, J. S. 1 00	Dickerson, David 2 00		Newbold, W. H., & Son &} 10 00
Butcher, Washington } 5 00	Drexel, A. J. 50 00	Jeanes, Isaac 5 00	Aertsen }
& Sons ....}	Disston, Charles 10 00	Jeanes, Joshua T. 10 00	Naylor, Jacob. 10 00
Bradshaw, James T. 5 00	Dwier, D. 5 00	Jeanes, Joseph 10 00	Norcross & Sheets 5 00
Beckhaus, Jos. 10 00	Eighth National Bank.... 10 00	Jeanes, Samuel 10 00	Norris, T. C. 5 00
Benners, H. B. 5 00	Eva, William T. 5 00	Jeanes, Mary 5 00	Noble, Joseph 2 00
Biddle Hardware Co. 10 00	Fitler, E. H. & Co. 10 00	Jeanes, Anna T 5 00	
Brady & Shafer 5 00	Flanagan, S. & J. M. 10 00	Jones, Jacob. 2 00	Orne, J. F. & E. B. 5 00
Blanchard, William A. ... 5 00	Fitler, W. 5 00	Jenks, William 5 00	Ogle, Mr. 1 00
Bohlen, Henry & Co. 5 00	Farrell, Herring & Co...... 5 00	Jones, E. 2 00	
Bacon, Joseph 10 00	Fisher, Peter. 2 00		Philad'a Iron & Steel Co.. 10 00
	Fincher, A. H. 2 00	Kent, James, Santee & Co. 5 00	Pardee, A. & Co 20 00
Chambers, A. R. Estate... 12 67	Fannon, Isaac 5 00	Keen & Coates 10 00	Powers, Thomas H. 10 00
Coleman, Robert M. 5 00	Garrison, David R. 100 00	Kesler, H. & G. 10 00	Patterson & Lippincott.... 5 00
Cattell, A. G. & Co 10 00	Gibson, John, Son & Co... 20 00	Knight, E. C. & Co. 5 00	Phila. & Reading R. R. Co. 50 00
Cope, Alfred 20 00	Geiger, A. J. 10 00	Kesler, Henry 2 00	Porter & Dickey 5 00
Cope Brothers 20 00	Gaskill, J. W. & Sons...... 5 00	Kensin'n M. E. Church,} 10 24	Paxson, Joseph 2 00
Cash, (E. N.) 20 00	Gillender & Sons 5 00	½ proceeds of collec. }	
Clark, E. W. & Co. 10 00	Gay, John 5 00		Robbins, Stephen 10 00
Childs, Geo. W. 20 00	Galvin, T. P. & Co. 5 00	Lewis, John T. & Bro...... 20 00	Rowland, James & Co..... 10 00
Child, Isaac K. 4 00	Gans, Arnold & Co 5 00	Landenberger, M. & Co... 10 00	Rihl, H. (M. D.) 10 00
Cramp, W. & Sons 25 00	Godey, L. A. 10 00	Leibrandt & McDowell.... 20 00	Riegel, Jacob & Co......... 10 00
Croskey, Henry & Co. 5 00		Lechler, A. J. 5 00	Ralquel, W. 1 00
Coates, Benjamin 5 00		Leaming, W. A. 5 00	Rowland, Wm. & Harvey 10 00
		Love, John B. 10 00	Rotan, W. H. 5 00
		Lewis S. Morris 5 00	Robbins, John 2 00
		Lea, Henry C. 5 00	Remick, E. (½ cost of)} 1 50
		Lippincott, Jos. 2 00	shade }
		Lukens, C. M. 2 00	Stoddart, C. & Bro. 5 00
		Larue, Albert 1 00	Schofield & Brauson 5 00
		Manderson, James 5 00	Souder & Adams 5 00
		Moore, Ellis P. & Co....... 5 00	Smith, Mahlon N. & Co... 5 00
		McBride, P. 5 00	Smylie, John 25 00
		Matthews, L. 5 00	Stockham, George 10 00
		Mason, Ann 5 00	Scott, Hamilton 5 00
		Mccutcheon, S. M. 2 00	Smith, T. J. 10 00
		Montgomery, T. M. 2 00	Sloan, H. & Sons 5 00

Contributors list, as shown in the Soup Society's 1873–74 annual report. The list is a who's who of Kensington and Fishtown businesses. *Kensington Soup Society Archives.*

One of the last newspaper reports found before the society's meeting minute ledgers take up their history was discovered in the *Philadelphia Inquirer* on February 26, 1874. The society stated that it was "doing good work in the way of taking care of the suffering and worthy poor." It was now "distributing daily 8,840 pints of soup to 413 families, consisting of 2,065 adults and children, and every other day they distribute 2,000 loaves of bread, besides feeding daily from 30 to 40 wayfarers." The soup was given out at eleven o'clock daily. The Soup Society also now added "coal" to the list of contributions that it was looking for people to contribute.

Besides documenting the pre-1875 years of the Soup Society, these newspaper articles in the local papers were also a good means of getting the word out to neighborhood folks to let them know that the soup was ready.

GETTING THE WORD OUT

The Soup House had various methods of getting out the word that the society was open for business or in need of foodstuffs or money. Besides the normal "word of mouth" throughout the neighborhood, the society also took out advertisements in local Philadelphia newspapers.

In the days before radio and television, newspapers were the most important medium for announcing the opening of the Soup House for the season or for the Annual Contributors Meeting, where nominations and elections for the Board of Managers were held. These announcements all took place between the third week of November and first two or three weeks of December. Later, during the season, there would occasionally be other advertisements announced, such as whether the society was sponsoring fundraisers, had emergency needs or for word of the final closing of the Soup House for the season.

Looking at the period of the 1870s, a period rich in receipts for the society's advertising efforts, we see that the Kensington's Soup Society paid for numerous advertisements in the local papers. For example, during the season of 1876–77, newspapers like Morton McMichael's the *North American*, George W. Childs's the *Public Ledger*, John W. Forney's the *Press* or School and Blakely's the *Evening Star* all ran advertisements for the Soup Society during the second week of December announcing the results of the elections of the Annual Contributors Meeting held the previous week. The old *Philadelphia Evening Bulletin* and even today's *Philadelphia Inquirer*, both of which were in business in the nineteenth century, also had paid advertisements that season for Kensington's Soup House, as did another paper, the *Times*, the "second most circulated morning paper in Philadelphia." In addition, the *Age*, another morning paper published by Robb and Biddle, carried the Soup Society's advertisements in the 1870s. It was a great period for Philadelphia newspapers as readers had a plentiful choice, unlike today, when there is only one.

Later in the mid-twentieth century, when local neighborhood newspapers sprung up like the *News*, a paper published by the Community Council of the eighteenth ward, the Soup Society would publish in these types of neighborhood newspapers as well.

At one point in the society's history (December 1953), when it was seeking a "stewardess assistant" for the Soup House, the society advertised in the *Ukrainian Daily Paper*, presumably because there was a high likelihood of finding a solid worker among the newer immigrants. The advertisement stated that the society wanted a "single or unencumbered" woman for the job.

Other ways that people heard about the Soup Society came in the way of the specially printed matter for the Soup Society, given out to prospective contributors to the Soup Society or to the recipients of soup. The 1870s were a plentiful period in the society's receipts for this sort of information. During this time, the society used a number of printers in the Northern Liberties and Center City. From 1870 to 1876, George S. Harris & Son, Steam Power Printers, at Fourth and Vine Streets, was used for the printing of circulars, cards and tickets, usually printing up to one thousand tickets, six hundred circulars or five hundred cards at a time, once or twice a season.

The tickets and circulars that were printed would be distributed throughout the neighborhood. The circulars advertised the Soup House and the tickets usually were given out to deserving families. Also, other charitable groups would receive tickets and they would give them to needy individuals for redemption at the Soup House. The cards that were printed were the "appeals" cards that were sent to people soliciting donations to the Soup Society. John Boyle, at Second and Green Streets, a printer of plain and ornamental jobs, was one such printer hired for this sort of printing.

For the annual reports of 1873–74 and 1874–75, the society looked to the better-known Center City printer E.C. Markley & Son at 422 Library Street. Library Street ran from Fourth to Fifth Street, below Chestnut, and it was a well-known place for higher-end printers.

There were also several local printers who were hired for different purposes. Richard Chapman of 935 North Second Street was used for purchasing "made to order blank books," sheet blotter, envelopes, pens, pencils and other stationery needs. In 1880, Moyer & Lesher at 249 Richmond Street printed up order blanks, tickets and heavy manila envelopes for the society. In 1950, seventy years later, we see that the Soup Society was still using Van Aken Printing Company of 223 East Girard Avenue, formerly Moyer & Lesher. In the twentieth century, the society also used Center City printer William F. Murphy's Sons Company, a commercial stationery and job printer.

It is unclear why the society used so many different printers. Perhaps it was a mere matter of cost or the types of printing jobs needed, or perhaps the society could spread around its printing cost needs and at the same time solicit the various printers for donations to the society.

A THREE-YEAR LOOK AT SOUP DISTRIBUTION
IN THE LATE 1870S

While the newspaper stories and reports by the Soup Society from the 1860s and early 1870s are informative, they do not compare to a full reporting of the Soup House's operations, or who visited the soup house and how the place operated. However, a look at the earliest available meeting minute ledgers does help to give insight into the daily operations of the Soup House and to understand the full scope of the Soup House's operations.

Table 3, shown below, compares the complete statistics for the first three seasons for which the reports of the House Committee are complete. The monthly minute ledgers for the Kensington Soup Society's Board of Managers' meetings start in November 1875, and while there are loose sheets for a few meetings in the 1860s and early 1870s, the first full season of complete reports of the Soup Society's meetings starts with the ledger for the years 1875 to 1899.

Taking a look at the first three seasons of these ledgers gives us some idea of the amount of soup distribution and the amount of people who were seeking charity, as well as the story of how the visitor position came to be created. These years are also important to examine as they had repercussions of the Panic of 1873, which ushered in an economic depression that affected many countries of the world and lasted as late as 1896. This period of economic history is often referred to as the "Long Depression."

TABLE 3: Comparison of the first three seasons (1875–78) of soup distribution, where complete statistics are available for the Kensington Soup Society.

	1875–76	1876–77	1877–78
Pints of Soup	60,790	143,272	110,200
Loaves of Bread	100	25,941	11,439
Families Supplied	3,504	5,536	3,932
Adults and Children	17,280	27,792	19,665
Wayfarers	1,596	2,123	5,004

During the season 1875–76, the Soup House opened on December 21, 1875, and closed on March 18, 1876. This time period represented twelve

An 1877 letter from Henry Disston, the great saw works manufacturer, asking that Kensington coordinate better with the Northern District Soup Society when serving residents. *Kensington Soup Society Archives.*

weeks during which the Soup House was open for six days a week, closing on Sundays. In general, the season ran twelve weeks, although some years it remained open a little longer.

The Honorable John Robbins, the president of the Soup Society, was present for the initial meeting of the year on November 19, 1875. After this initial meeting, he then missed all sixteen meetings between that date and the next season's first meeting on November 24, 1876, including the annual meeting of December 2, 1875, where he was nominated and elected again as the president. Perhaps, like many nonprofit organizations today, Robbins was simply a figurehead, elected for the prestige of having a U.S. congressman on the Board of Managers, or possibly elected to have someone who may have had access to potential contributors to the society.

Robbins served in Congress from March 4, 1849, until March 3, 1855, and was then reelected and served from March 4, 1875, to March 3, 1877, which is the time frame that parallels the period of his presidency of the Soup Society. It may be that Robbins was in Washington, D.C., during that winter of 1875–76 and that is why he attended no meetings.

Table 4 below lists the figures for the winter of 1875–76, showing the amount of soup given out by the Soup House and the number of people served during that season.

TABLE 4: Figures for the winter of 1875–76.

Opened: December 21, 1875
Closed: March 18, 1876

Week	1	2	3	4	5	6
Pints of Soup Given Out	530	4,120	6,680	6,240	5,960	6,240
Loaves of Bread	0	100	0	0	0	0
Families Supplied	94	177	226	249	270	280
Adults and Children	487	973	1,320	1,245	1,350	865
Wayfarers	0	24	106	93	95	118

The Soup House in the Late Nineteenth Century

Week	7	8	9	10	11	12
Pints of Soup Given Out	6,240	5,580	5,200	5,600	4,560	3,840
Loaves of Bread	0	0	0	0	0	0
Families Supplied	149	169	157	300	744	690
Adults and Children	745	845	785	1,500	3,720	3,450
Wayfarers	171	189	147	183	138	330

The opening week of the Soup House started slowly, as might be expected. The society would advertise the opening date for the season in the local newspapers (*Public Ledger*, *Philadelphia Bulletin*, *Philadelphia Inquirer*, as well as several others) and it took a week or two for the society to advertise enough to the point where the needy started to show up in large numbers.

In the first week, only ninety-four families showed up for soup. In the second week of the season, the Soup House, perhaps as a way to promote its activities, gave away one hundred loaves of bread, which increased attendance by 188 percent. Thereafter, no more loaves were given out, except for bread with the soup, several times a week.

During the tenth week, there were eighteen bushels of potatoes given out. This may explain the spike in the number of families being served for that week and the week after (weeks ten and eleven), when it went from 169 families in week 9, to 300 in week 10, to 744 families in week 11, when they gave out potatoes. Presumably, the season was winding down and the Soup House had some perishable foodstuffs left over that were not returnable, so they needed to be given away before it closed for the season.

The high numbers came again the following week (week twelve), the last week of the season, particularly among the wayfarers. There was an increase of over 225 percent among this demographic, as either they got word that potatoes were given out the previous week or they knew that it was the last week of the season, a time when societies gave away their perishable items. However, there were no bushels of potatoes for distribution when the season ended.

These houses stood on the west side of Thompson Street, north of Columbia Avenue. They show some of the poverty within the community.

For the year 1875–76, there were 60,790 pints of soup given out, or an average of 5,066 per week. The average number of families that came each week was 292. The average number of adults and children that composed those 292 families amounted to 1,440 per week. Factoring in the average 133 wayfarers who showed up each week, the Soup House distributed approximately 3.2 pints of soup per week per person. Since the Soup House was open six days a week (no Sundays), the average amount of soup would come to a little more then a half pint per day per person, or a large cup of soup a day, with a piece of bread.

The numbers for wayfarers were kept separate from adults and children. The wayfarers coming to the Soup House averaged 133 per week, with the lightest turnouts in the first couple of weeks (0 in week one and 24 in the second week) and the heaviest in the last week, when 300 turned up. This possibly indicates that the wayfarers, perhaps not regular newspaper readers or necessarily living in the proximity of the Soup House, found out through the "hobo grapevine" that the Soup House was open and eventually started to trickle in by week three.

The Soup House in the Late Nineteenth Century

The fact that so many wayfarers showed up in the last week of the season seems to indicate that the practice of Soup Houses giving away perishables at the end of the season was a well-known fact. As we saw in 1875–76, the Kensington Soup Society gave away potatoes on the next to last week of the season, perhaps knowing in advance that the wayfarers would crowd the place in the last week. Thus, it avoided giving away the potatoes to the wayfarers, whom they considered the "undeserving poor," and were able to give to the local families who were truly in need.

The 1876–77 season was busier than the previous season. The amount of soup given out during the twelve-week season was 145,384 pints, along with 25,941 loaves of bread. There were 5,536 families supplied comprising 27,792 adults and children. This season also saw 2,123 wayfarers. The average attendance at the Soup House was 2,301 people a week, making the charitable distribution about 11,020 pints of soup and 2,953 loaves of bread a week. These statistics seem to show that each person would have received almost 5 pints of soup a week, or just under 1 pint a day. They would also receive a piece of bread a day, or a little over a loaf a week.

The 1875–76 season had 1,440 people each week seeking charity, plus an additional 133 wayfarers showing up per week. The very next year, the 1876–77 season, the number of individuals served increased by 861, with the wayfarers total increasing by 30 per week. Thus, with more people seeking charity, the Kensington Soup Society more than doubled its production of soup from the previous year, found money for more bread and enabled the people to receive on average a bigger cup of soup than the previous year. Without its new home at the Crease Street location, it is doubtful that the Kensington Soup Society could have filled the needs of the community.

Compared to 1876–77, the 1877–78 season saw a decrease in just about all areas. The number of families and individuals decreased, which caused a reduction in the production of soup by 33,000 pints, as well as a decrease in the distribution of bread by over 14,000 loaves. However, while family numbers decreased from 27,792 down to 19,665, the number of wayfarers more then doubled, from 2,123 to 5,005.

Some of the decrease of families coming to the Soup House may be due to the fact that in February 1878, the various soup societies that shared borders with Kensington (North East, Richmond and Northern) sent representatives of their respective societies to a meeting held to adjust boundaries. Kensington's new boundaries became: from the Delaware River west on Laurel Street to second Street, north on Second Street to Oxford Street, east on Oxford Street to Frankford Road, north on Frankford Road to Vienna

(Berks) Street, east on Vienna Street to Cedar Street, north on Cedar Street to Gunner's Run (Aramingo Avenue), from Gunner's Run southeast to the Delaware River and then south on the river to Laurel Street.

THE CREATION OF THE VISITOR POSITION

Because of the steep increase in wayfarers showing up on the steps of the Soup House, the society took action at its annual meeting of December 19, 1878, for "better protection of the Society against imposition" by creating a five-man committee to study the issue. The previous March, the society had considered attending a meeting to which the board was invited in order to "consider an intelligent economical and effective application of the charitable contribution of the city of Philadelphia and the prevention of the pauperism and vice engaged by the present loose unguarded and conflicting modes of aid giving, etc." The end result of these meetings, in continuation with the reports of the Committee of Five, was the creation by the Kensington Soup Society of the visitor position.

No.............................

Philadelphia,..191.....

The Kensington Soup Society of Philadelphia,

1036 CREASE STREET,

Will please furnish Soup for ....

Residence, ...

whose family consists....................Adults, and................Children.

The soup form for a family to receive soup from the society. The society issued these to be redeemed by families for soup and bread. *Kensington Soup Society Archives.*

The visitor would call on all potential applicants recommended to him by an investigative committee of the board. These applicants would be investigated to determine if they were actually worthy of the society's support. The visitor would make sure the applicant was not "double dipping" by living outside the borders of the society. Double dippers were those who received support from their neighborhood soup society and at the same time tried to get support from the Kensington Soup Society.

Another responsibility of the visitor was to make sure that the applicants were not "bummers," single men or hobos with no permanent residence or job who simply wanted handouts and were not considered to be part of the "worthy poor."

This new position of visitor would help the Soup Society weed out those wayfarers who were not part of the "worthy poor."

Bread Every Day

Board of Managers member Oakley Cowdrick was hired as the first visitor. While Cowdrick was out on the streets visiting households in this position, the poverty of the families that he visited must have had an effect on him. In a meeting of February 21, 1879, Cowdrick filed a motion that bread should be given out every day. However, his motion was tabled by treasurer George J. Hamilton and was eventually defeated at the next meeting.

The issue of "daily bread distribution" was again taken up on January 22, 1880. However, this time it was W.W. Taxis who introduced the resolution, but again it was tabled. On February 5, 1880, Board of Managers member Benjamin R. Bacon introduced a motion for daily bread to be given out, but the society's tightfisted treasurer, Hamilton, stymied the motion once more. Eventually, Hamilton amended Bacon's resolution, with the final result that bread was given out three times a week. This practice was adopted for the time being.

At the next meeting of the Board of Managers on February 12, 1880, Jacob Jones proposed that bread be given out every day. Finally, after a year's discussion, the board was able to come to an agreement and it was voted that bread would be given out every day.

Since the amount of bread given out more then doubled from $325\frac{1}{2}$ pounds on February 12, 1880, to 680 pounds as reported on February 26, 1880, we can see why giving bread out every day was such an issue. The cost involved doubled with daily distribution, from $11.39 to $23.80. While these monetary figures do not appear that large today, the value of that $11.39 in the year 1880 would today be approximately $225.00 (consumer price index) to $1,500.00 (unskilled labor wage index), so doubling from $450.00 to $3,000.00 is substantial. Hamilton, as the treasurer of the society, would be responsible for justifying this increased expenditure of the society; thus, his objections to the motion of increasing the bread giveaways would appear the natural thing for him to do.

The issue of daily bread distribution was a point that would continue to surface at meetings. It was revisited and discussed almost every year, with various results. Sometimes bread was given out every day, every other day or even three times a week, all within the same season. It would generally depend upon the demand and the finances of the treasury for any given season.

A STEADY SUPPLY OF VENDORS

In order to operate the day-to-day business of the Soup House, the society needed good, reliable vendors whom they could count on for supplying them with the meat, vegetables and other food products necessary for making soup. The society relied on local as well as downtown vendors.

One of the earliest receipts that still exists (in the form of a letterhead) is from Barker & Co., a produce commission merchant at 238 North Delaware Avenue. This order, dated December 29, 1869, shows Barker selling the Soup House barrels of beans and onions as well as bushels of potatoes. This company had at least a ten-year (1869–79) business relationship with the Soup Society.

Joseph Wilkinson & Co., at Pier 8½ North Delaware Avenue, a fruit and produce dealer, seems to have been the main bean supplier to the Soup House for the better part of the 1870s. The Soup House also dealt with local vendor Fling, Shrigley & Co., of 811 and 819 North Second Street, for fruit and produce, and with Richards & Culin at Tenth and Arch Streets when it needed "sweet marjoram."

Another local vendor the Soup House used was W.J. Heiss & Bro. at Front and Girard. This company was a wholesale grocer and appears to have been the Soup House's supplier for pepper and kegs of barley. Heiss & Bro. did business with the Soup House throughout the 1870s and into the 1880s.

The flour vendor for the Soup House in the early 1870s was Detwiler & Hartranft, at 1015 North Delaware Avenue. Frederick Kramer, a local baker from Richmond Street, was the Soup House's baker in the first half of the

Joseph H. Schiedt, a local beef butcher who operated a stall at the East Girard Avenue Market, supplied meat to the Kensington Soup Society, 1879. *Kensington Soup Society Archives.*

1870s, providing it with loaves of bread from 1870 to 1875. Thomas Gould, a baker on Vienna (Berks) Street, supplied the Soup Society during the late 1870s and early 1880s.

One local butcher at the East Girard Avenue Market found a customer in the Soup House. Joseph H. Schiedt, a beef butcher who had stall 17, section 52, at the East Girard Avenue Market, sold hundreds of pounds of beef to the Soup Society in the late 1870s. Benjamin Saeltzer, a dealer in "Fresh & Dried Beef, Tongues, &c." had several contracts with the Soup House in the 1870s. Saeltzer had stalls 8 and 10 at the Second Street Market, down along Second Street between Brown and Poplar Streets. The Soup House usually tried to contract for a guaranteed seasonal price with a butcher. Besides Schiedt, the Soup Society also contracted for meat in the 1870s with local butchers R.B. Vaughan, Charles P. Fisher of Belgrade Street and Alexander McCoy, another Girard Avenue Market vendor. A weekly order with one of these vendors in the 1870s might have been for three to four hundred pounds of beef.

Besides using local vendors and vendors from nearby neighborhoods, the Kensington Soup Society also used and solicited vendors who sat on the society's own Board of Managers. Joseph Bennett, a local grocer and early Board of Managers member at the Soup Society's incorporation in 1853, sold the Soup House bushels of salt in 1871. Another member of the Board of Managers who had business transactions with the Soup Society was a

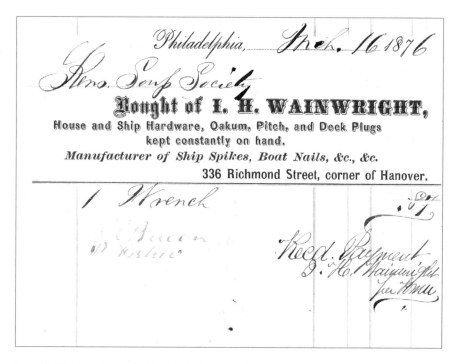

Plumber Samuel Smeeton, 206 Richmond Street, serviced the Soup House in the 1870s. In 1890, he joined the Board of Managers of the Soup Society. *Kensington Soup Society Archives.*

Isaac H. Wainwright, on the Board of Managers for seventeen years, also did private business with the Soup Society, including this invoice for 1876. *Kensington Soup Society Archives.*

former vice-president and president. Edward W. Gorgas was a Kensington lumberman located at 1325 Beach Street, at the third wharf above Hanover (Columbia) Street. From March 1879 to February 1882 we find Gorgas selling cords of lumber to the Soup House during the time he held the vice-president's and president's offices.

For the decade of January 1871 to December 1881, Samuel Smeeton, plumber and gas fitter, of 961 Shackamaxon Street (later 207 Richmond Street), billed the Soup Society for various jobs ranging from two dollars to over thirty dollars. The tasks varied from minor soldering jobs to larger jobs involving two men and material for work on the Soup House's kitchen. Through the work his company was doing for the Soup House, Smeeton would appear to have been drawn into the society. In 1890, he joined the Board of Managers and in 1900 became the vice-president; the very next year, he became president, a position he held from 1901 to 1908.

The Wainwright family, an old Kensington hardware and ship chandler family, had a number of transactions with the Soup House between November 1874 and July 1879. The Wainwrights sold hardware to the Soup House (wrench, shovel, gallon scuttle), as well as lumber. The family had several businesses in Kensington. Their house and ship hardware business was at 336 Richmond Street, at the corner of Hanover (Columbia Avenue). The Wainwright and Bryant lumber wharf was at the corner of Beach and Hanover and at the Hanover Street Wharf. Two members of the family, Richard Wainwright and J.H. Wainwright, served on the Board of Managers of the Soup Society.

Longtime Soup Society collector David Dickerson also had business dealings with the Soup House. In addition to the commissions that Dickerson made during his tenure as the society's collector (1875–1904), he also had a paperhanging business at 235 (later 339) Richmond Street, and the records show that on at least three occasions in the 1870s (before and after Dickerson was on the Board of Managers of the Soup Society) Dickerson was hired by the society to paper the Soup House. He performed a major job in December 1872, presumably soon after the society opened the new Soup House. There were two smaller jobs in 1876 and 1877. The large contract that Dickerson received from the society in 1872 might have induced Dickerson to join the Board of Managers in the fall of 1873. He went on to serve the Board for thirty-three years.

William C. Mohler, a longtime member of the Board of Managers (1881–1910), also had business transactions with the Soup Society. In addition to serving as the longtime visitor (1884–88, 1893–1902) and collector (1904–10), in which job he collected fees and commission for his duties, Mohler was also a wholesale and retail dealer in flour, grain, hay, straw, cake meal and mill feed. For the period from December 1876 to January 1880, Mohler had a regular business relationship with the Soup House, selling it flour for six dollars a barrel. The business receipts stop in January 1880, roughly ten months before Mohler was elected to the Board of Managers of the Soup Society. Mohler, like Samuel Smeeton, appears to have been recruited onto the Board of Managers of the Soup Society through his company's business relationship with the Soup House.

Later in the twentieth century, Edward L. Corner, a Board of Managers member and a one-time president of the society, sold general merchandise to the Soup Society. Hose, blankets and bedspreads were supplied to the society from his general merchandise business at 1100 North Delaware Avenue.

BANKING AND PAYING THE VENDORS

Like any business organization, the Soup Society needed a trusted associate in the banking industry. The bank of the Soup Society was the local Kensington National Bank, the oldest bank in Kensington. The bank, founded in 1826, was first located on the 900 block of Beach Street before relocating to the southeast corner of Frankford and Girard Avenues in 1878. This bank had an excellent record for having paid a dividend for just about every year of its existence.

The Soup Society's president, the Honorable John Robbins (who presided over the Soup Society as president for the years 1872 to 1880), was also a former director and president of Kensington National Bank. William C.

A Soup Society check drawn on the Kensington National Bank. Many Soup Society directors also served as directors of this bank, 1875. *Kensington Soup Society Archives.*

The Kensington National Bank, the bankers for the Kensington Soup Society, had a number of directors who also served on the Soup Society's Board of Managers.

Williamson, John D. Williamson Jr. and William F. Sauter were all directors of the bank and, at one time, members of the Board of Managers of the Soup Society.

The available records of the Soup Society reveal that the society had an account at Kensington National Bank from as early as August 1870 (probably much earlier). In 1948, the Pennsylvania Company for Banking and Trusts (First Pennsylvania Trust) took over the old Kensington National Bank. The society continued banking with this new bank.

Payments for the Soup Society's expenses were drawn on the bank by the society's treasurer and paid for with checks. The treasurers of the Soup Society, people like George J. Hamilton, William W. Taxis, George Kessler, I.P.H. Wilmerton and James R. Anderson, handled the writing of the checks and payment of the bills. At least one of the treasurers, James R. Anderson, was a stockholder in the Kensington National Bank, and it is likely that a number of the other Board of Managers over the years were as well.

The longtime secretary of the Soup Society, Thomas M. Montgomery (a partner in Lukens & Montgomery, conveyancers), was the public notary for the bank.

CHAPTER 6

The Williamson Family
and Coal Fund

The Soup Society's Williamson Family

The Williamson family played a large role in the Soup Society's history. There were at least five members of this family who served on the Board of Managers: three brothers (George W., John D. and William C.), a son of one of the brothers (William C.'s son, John D. Jr.) and a son-in-law of one of the brothers (Harry W. Hand, who married William C.'s daughter Lizzie). One of the brothers, John D. Williamson, held the Soup Society's presidency for the years 1909 until 1919, when he died. This John D. Williamson is also the same person who started the Williamson Coal Fund, which provided the needy of Kensington with coal during the winter months. By examining the Williamson family, we can get a picture of an American success story and also see what sort of men were responsible for governing the Soup Society and how their philanthropy benefited the many residents of Kensington.

James Williamson, the patriarch of the family, was born about 1790 in Ireland and died between 1850 and 1860. He first appears in Kensington as a grocer as early as 1830. His wife Mary (also born in Ireland) was born about the year 1789 and died in 1879. The couple had four children, three boys (George, John and William) and one girl (Margaret). Margaret was born in Pennsylvania in 1822, so the family appears to have immigrated by at least that year.

Between 1830 and 1860, the Williamson family lived in the western section of the then self-governing district of Kensington, the second and third wards (between Front and Sixth Streets, north of the old Cohocksink Creek and south of Montgomery Avenue).

George W. was the oldest son, born about 1829. He served on the Board of Managers of the Soup Society during the years 1888 to 1896. Of the three brothers, he was the least active, despite his eight years of service. He was the first brother to marry and move out of the family home. In 1870, he was shown living at 1358 Richmond Street and listed as working as a machinist. Later, in 1880, he is found living at 1334 Montgomery Avenue, an address where he lived until he died on March 26, 1896, at the age of sixty-seven. His estate at his death was said to be over $100,000, or in today's dollars approximately $2,500,000.

The next youngest child was John D. Williamson. He appears to have been the last of the three brothers to be married. By 1870, John, a master machinist, moved with his widowed mother to his sister and brother-in-law's house, the retired grocer James Kennedy, who lived in the twenty-fourth ward.

By 1880, John had married and moved back to Kensington, to 1520 Palmer Street. The 1890 Philadelphia city directory shows Williamson had moved to 1134 Shackamaxon Street, where he lived until at least 1910, if not until his death. He was seventy-five years old in 1910 when he retired.

John D. Williamson died in early March 1919. His nephew, John D. Williamson Jr., handled his estate. He had served on the Kensington Soup Society's Board of Managers from 1882 until his death in 1919. He became the president of the Soup Society in 1908 and served in that capacity until his death. He had previously been vice-president from 1901 to 1908. He also served on the Real Estate Committee for the years 1892–94, 1897–98 and 1900–09. When the Board of Managers was split in 1911 between managers and auxiliary managers, he remained one of the managers. His legacy was continued by the creation of the John D. Williamson Coal Fund.

William C. Williamson, the youngest of the three brothers and the father of John D. Williamson Jr., was born in September 1837 in Delaware, the only one of the boys born outside Pennsylvania. By 1870, William had moved out of his mother's home and lived in Kensington, working as a machinist engineer. He had married and had two children. His son John is the John D. Williamson Jr. who would eventually join the Soup Society's Board of Managers.

In the census of 1880, the family lived at 1021 Hanover (Columbia) Street. By 1890, the Philadelphia city directory shows that William C. Williamson lived at 1800 North Sixteenth Street, the "new money" neighborhood of

North Broad Street, where many native Kensington manufacturers moved to once they became successful.

By the time the census of 1900 was taken, William had moved again, this time farther out, to Cheltenham Township, Montgomery County, Pennsylvania, where he and his family lived until they all passed away. Lizzie Williamson, William's daughter, married Harry W. Hand and lived with William C. at his Cheltenham Township home. Harry W. Hand also served on the Kensington Soup Society board.

After William retired, he continued to live in Cheltenham with his daughter and son-in-law, who cared for him after the death of his wife in 1910. William C. Williamson died on December 2, 1916, and was buried with his wife at Laurel Hill Cemetery.

Harry W. Hand, William C.'s son-in-law, served on the Board of Managers of the Soup Society from 1911 until at least 1923. He always was listed as an advisory or auxiliary manager.

When the famed ship and engine builder Joseph G. Neafie died, William C. Williamson was an honorary pallbearer. C. Wesley Ruffell, a Board of Managers member of the Kensington Soup Society, was one of the "official" pallbearers.

William C. Williamson was the first of the Williamson family to associate with the Kensington Soup Society. He was elected to the Board of Managers in 1878 and continuously served until he died in 1916. During that time,

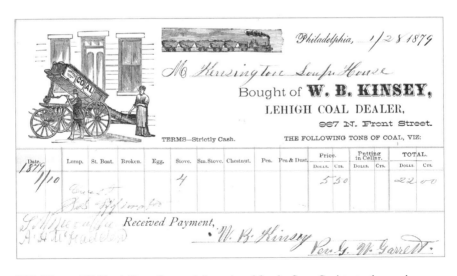

W.B. Kinsey, 967 North Front Street, delivered coal for the Soup Society to the needy families in the early 1870s. *Kensington Soup Society Archives.*

he served on the Committee on Distribution Protection (1878–79) and the Committee on Entertainment (1882–83). When the Board of Managers was split into managers and advisory managers in 1911, he served as an advisory, or auxiliary, manager from that time until he died in 1916.

William C.'s son, John D. Williamson Jr., is found in 1920 listed as a retired mechanical engineer. He was only fifty-four years old, but appears to have taken an early retirement. He and his wife Marion lived on Old York Road in Cheltenham Township, Montgomery County. John D. Williamson Jr. was first elected to the Soup Society's Board of Managers in 1911 and served continuously until 1942. He was always listed as either an advisory or auxiliary manager. When John D. Williamson Jr.'s involvement in the Soup Society ceased in 1942, it brought to an end a sixty-four-year involvement of the Williamson family in the society's Board of Managers.

PERSEVERANCE IRON WORKS, AKA WILLIAMSON BROS. CO.

The three Williamson brothers started in business as early as 1867, at the Perseverance Iron Works, located on East York Street between Salmon and Richmond Streets. It later became known simply as Williamson Bros. Co. The company could not have started much earlier than 1867, as William C. and his brother John D. were both naval engineers who served in the military during the Civil War. William mustered out in 1866, his brother John in 1865.

William C. Williamson served in the U.S. Navy for the entire duration of the war, from February 19, 1861, until January 10, 1866. Promoted from third assistant engineer (midshipman) to second assistant engineer (ensign), he finally resigned as a first assistant engineer (master) and was honorably discharged.

John D. Williamson started out as acting second assistant engineer (midshipman) on December 2, 1861, was promoted to acting first assistant engineer (ensign) and then acting chief engineer (lieutenant commander) when he was honorably discharged on October 2, 1865.

With their backgrounds as machinists and the engineering skills they acquired in naval science, the two brothers became master machinists. The firm they created initially included them and their older brother, George W. Williamson. Later on, they added John D. Williamson Jr., William C.'s oldest son.

A Hexemer Insurance Survey completed in the 1880s stated that Williamson Bros. manufactured steam engines, hoisting engines and steering engines, and that the company employed sixty workers, including five boys. The machine shop was erected in 1882 and the auxiliary buildings in 1874. The plant was run by steam power and used raw stock of iron, brass and pattern lumber.

By 1883, Williamson Bros. Co., still on York Street, advertised that it could:

> *Manufacture Stationary and Marine Engines and Boilers of Every Description; Tanks, Sugar Cars, &c., Shafting, Gearing and Machinery in general. Patentees and Sold Manufacturers of Williamson Bros' Patent Frictional Geared Hosting Engines and Machines, specially adapted for Vessels, Wharves, Pile Drivers, Quarries, Factories, &c.*

The 1890 Philadelphia city directory shows Williamson Bros. (George W., John D. and William C.), machinists, as being located at 2735 East York Street. In 1902, the company contracted with William Steele & Sons to build a new plant for $100,000. It purchased a lot on the west side of Aramingo Avenue, 156 feet south of Cumberland, just north of York Street. Steele & Sons built a group of five buildings, consisting of two foundries (one 210 by 55 feet, the other 175 by 55 feet), one two-story brick storage and supply building and two three-story shipping and storage buildings.

As the company progressed, the brothers all became wealthy, so much so that in 1904, William C. and John D. Williamson contributed to a fund for Charles H. Cramp. He was having financial difficulties at his shipyard, owing various creditors over $335,000. The fund was created to protect the shares of Cramp Shipyard stock owned by Charles H. Cramp so that his creditors could not take control of the stock or the company.

THE JOHN D. WILLIAMSON COAL FUND

The year 1909 saw the establishment of the John D. Williamson Coal Fund. Williamson was nominated president of the Soup Society in 1909, but he asked to be excused and instead donated $100 for the distribution of coal. The society kindly accepted his monetary donation but decided to elect him to the presidency anyway. The following year, he again donated $100 for coal for the needy, and his gift became an annual tradition for the rest of his life.

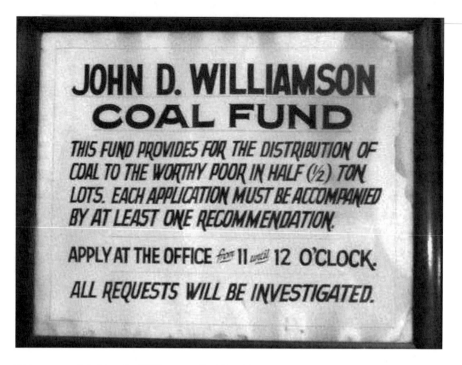

This poster advertising the Williamson Coal Fund hung on the Soup House's wall from the time the fund started (1909) until the year 2008. *Kensington Soup Society Archives.*

In 1916, James R. Anderson became secretary pro tem to replace the aging secretary, Thomas M. Montgomery. After Anderson was elected secretary the following year, he did not keep records as accurately as Montgomery had, one from the "old school" tradition. The Soup Society's minutes for some years included a separate accounting for the Williamson Coal Fund, but with Anderson's service as secretary, this practice stopped. It appears that an amount of $4,750 might have been given to the coal fund once John D. Williamson died and his estate was probated. That would be about $90,000 in today's money.

The coal fund was set up to help the "deserving poor" of Kensington stay warm in the cold winter months. The usual delivery was one half or one ton of coal, either "pea" or "nut." The usual recipient was a woman, perhaps a widow, or a family whose husband was out of work, lame or both. A number of receipts have been saved and are in the archives of the Soup Society. For the decade of the 1940s, these receipts were generally approved by John Radcliffe, the superintendent, and Edward Corner, the president, and paid for with a check drawn on the Kensington National Bank.

The Williamson Family and Coal Fund

Frederick and Dorothea Trinkler were part of the mass of German immigrants who crowded into the neighborhood surrounding the Kensington Soup Society in the nineteenth century.

JOHN D. WILLIAMSON

COAL FUND

KENSINGTON SOUP SOCIETY

1036 CREASE STREET

TRUSTEE

Philadelphia, ...192

You will receive Half a Ton of Pea Coal on

A Williamson Coal Fund card given to the needy of Kensington. It could be redeemed for coal in the amount that the Soup Society provided. *Kensington Soup Society Archives.*

The 1950s saw the Williamson Coal Fund deliveries continuing at their normal rate and the price of coal continuing to rise. In 1951, it was at $16.95 a ton, going up from $21.95 to $22.95 for a ton of "nut" by the end of the year and into 1953, with "pea" hovering from about $17.85 to $18.85 a ton going into the new year. By 1955–56, coal was selling at $13.50 for a half ton and appears to have stayed at that level or slightly higher for the rest of the 1950s.

While the Williamson Coal Fund was in operation, different institutions in the neighborhood wrote letters to the Soup Society asking for coal assistance for families in their care. Lutheran Settlement House at 1340 Frankford Avenue, St. Michael's Church at Second and Jefferson and Brethren in Christ Church, at 3415–19 North Second Street, were three such institutions, as was the Brotherhood Mission at 401–05 East Girard Avenue. In other cases, residents of the neighborhood might get their doctor, pharmacist or even their local schoolteachers to write a note stating that they were in need of coal.

We can assume that after the death of John D. Williamson in 1919, his nephew, John D. Williamson Jr., would have overseen the Williamson Coal Fund, as he continued on the Board of Managers until 1942; at that point, the fund presumably would have been managed by the Board of Managers.

The Williamson Family and Coal Fund

By 1963, after fifty-four years, the Williamson Coal Fund was finally reaching the end of its financial reserves. The rise of the welfare state in America provided other options for the destitute. As it is was reported by Charles F. Weeks in a Soup House report of April 4, 1963:

> *No coal was dispensed this season. Relative to the coal fund, only two casual inquiries were received. At the beginning of the season we were asked whether we were going to give coal this season. I am of the opinion that the reason for this change is due to the fact that some department of the City of Philadelphia maintains a spot at the Wills Eye Hospital to which the needy are directed by the local representative of Dept. of Public Assistance and shortly after registering, the coal is delivered. This information was confirmed by one of the recipients.*

CHAPTER 7

WORLD WAR I, THE GREAT DEPRESSION AND WORLD WAR II

During the presidency of John D. Williamson (1908–19), the Board of Managers of the Soup Society made a decision to begin printing appeals cards. The cards would be used as a form of advertisement for the society as well as a direct appeal to potential donors of the organization. The cards listed the officers of the society, along with a summary of the operation of the society for the previous winter. The address of the treasurer of the society was given in the event that a donor wished to send charitable contributions. The authorized collector for the society was listed with the address as well.

The appeals cards were distributed throughout the community to potential contributors and previous donors. The purpose was to indicate the amount of charity that was given out each year by the Soup Society. For the purposes of this study, these cards are very informative, as they give summaries of the work of the Soup Society for various years, in particular for the years of important episodes in American history, such as World War I and the Great Depression.

The appeals cards format was finalized at the Board of Managers meeting in November 1911 and began to be published at the end of the 1911–12 season. From the Soup Society's archives, it appears that these cards were printed from this time well into the 1930s. By analyzing these appeals, we can see the demands placed on the Soup Society during critical times in American history.

Israel P.H. Wilmerton (1840–1914), a local Columbia Avenue lumber merchant, served twenty-eight years on the Board of Managers, eight of those years as treasurer.

WORLD WAR I, 1914–1918

Any disruption in the American economy would usually affect the distribution of soup at the Kensington Soup House. Economic depressions or military crises brought on by domestic or foreign wars would usually mean that men were unemployed or husbands and fathers were away at war, and the need for charity would arise. This chapter surveys the two major wars of the twentieth century, as well as the Great Depression, the decade of the 1930s.

Table 5 below shows the distribution of charity by the Soup Society during the era of World War I (1914–18).

TABLE 5: Summary of operations of the Kensington Soup Society during the years immediately before and during World War I.

Type of Charity	1913–14	1914–15	1915–16	1916–17
No. of Loaves of Bread Distributed	22,619	41,421	25,940	21,694

World War I, the Great Depression and World War II

	1913–14	1914–15	1915–16	1916–17
No. of Pints of Soup Distributed	49,008	77,440	56,520	51,720
No. of Families	230	450	170	320
Daily Average no. of Families Supplied	123	230	151	110
No. of ½ Tons of Coal Distributed	43	51	38	35

While complete statistics are not available for the 1917–18 season, the last year of the war, we do know how much the Soup House distributed for the months of January and February 1918.

January 1918, the Soup House distributed the following:

Meat	627 pounds
Bread	4,090 loaves
Soup	1,785 gallons
People	50 per day on January 7, increasing to 90 for the last ten days of January
Families	21 per day on January 7, increasing to 77 by January 31

KENSINGTON SOUP SOCIETY

Chartered April 18, 1853

1036 CREASE STREET

Philadelphia, January 1, 1918

The Kensington Soup Society appeals to the charitable inclined for support of this Institution to carry on its work for the coming winter.

Donations, Checks or Money may be sent to the Society in care of the Treasurer, Mr. James R. Anderson, 1135 Shackamaxon Street.

Summary of the operation of the Society for the winter	1915-1916	1916-1917
No. of Loaves of Bread distributed	25,940	21,694
No. of Pints of Soup distributed	56,520	51,720
No. of Families supplied	170	320
Average No. of Families supplied	151	110
No. of ½ Tons of Coal distributed, by private contribution,	38	35

Mrs. Anna Wallace, 1130 E. Columbia Ave. is the authorized collector for the Society.

JOHN D. WILLIAMSON, President.   **EDWARD L. CORNER**, Vice President.

JAMES R. ANDERSON, Treasurer.   **THOS. M. MONTGOMERY**, Secretary.

Summary report for the years 1915 to 1917, showing the distribution of soup during World War I. *Kensington Soup Society Archives.*

February 1918, the Soup House distributed the following:

Meat	728 pounds
Bread	4,800 loaves, 200 each day
Soup	2,160 gallons, or 90 gallons each day
Families	78 per day

When compared to the distribution statistics of Table 5, these statistics for 1917–18 show that the needed supplies and services decreased as the war wound down.

THE GREAT DEPRESSION, 1929–1939

The next great event in the Soup House's history was the Great Depression, the result of an economic downturn initiated by the stock market crash of October 29, 1929. It began in the United States but soon spread to Europe and other parts of the world, particularly the industrialized countries. The Depression ended at different times in different countries. During the Depression, many countries set up relief programs, and in America, public assistance programs began. The beginning of these federal welfare programs in America was also the beginning of the decline of the Kensington Soup Society, as the federal government began to provide assistance to the poor, assisting them in their times of need.

The Great Depression that began in America was not a quick or sudden collapse. The economy gradually declined between October 1929 and March 1933. The year 1933 was the worst year of the Depression, and from that point the economy began to gradually recover until the recession of 1937. It was only with the outbreak of World War II in Europe that domestic and foreign rearmament demands caused the eventual long-term recovery of the economy and the ultimate end of the Depression.

After the death of John D. Williamson (the Soup Society's president) in 1919, the Board of Managers elected Edward L. Corner. It would be under the administration of Corner that the Soup Society would face the worst economic times in American history. Corner was president of the Soup Society from 1919 until his death on October 9, 1955.

As one can imagine, during an economic depression the need for general charity would be greatest, and the Soup House was no exception. The Kensington Soup Society's records reflect the economic ups and downs of the Depression-era days. The amount of charity given out in 1930–31

KENSINGTON SOUP SOCIETY

Chartered April 18th, 1853   1036 CREASE STREET

Philadelphia, December 6th, 1928.

The Kensington Soup Society appeals to the charitably inclined for support of this Institution to carry on its work for the coming winter.

Contributions for the work of the Society are needed and will be appreciated.

Donations, Checks or Money may be sent to the Society in care of the Treasurer, Mr. James R. Anderson, 1135 Shackamaxon Street.

Summary of the operation of the Society for the winter Dec. 19, 1927 to March 31, 1928 :

No. of Loaves of Bread distributed	16,495
No. of Pints of Soup distributed	85,080
No. of Families supplied	125
Average No. of Families supplied	90
No. of ½ Tons of Coal distributed by private contribution	56
Free Bowls of Soup (and Bread) to Needy Men	7,200

EDWARD L. CORNER, President   ALFRED CANNON, Vice-President

JAMES R. ANDERSON, Treasurer   LOUIS D. CASNER, Secretary

KENSINGTON SOUP SOCIETY

Chartered April 18th, 1853   1036 CREASE STREET

Philadelphia, April 5, 1931.

The Kensington Soup Society appeals to the charitably inclined for support of this Institution to carry on its work for the coming winter.

Contributions for the work of the society are needed and will be appreciated.

Donations, Checks or Money may be sent to the Society in care of the Treasurer, Mr. James R. Anderson, 1135 Shackamaxon Street.

Summary of the operation of the Society for the winter Dec. 1, 1930 to April 4, 1931:

No. of Loaves of Bread distributed	23,499
No. of Pints of Soup distributed	117,064
No. of Families supplied	298
Average No. of Families supplied	155
No. of Half Tons of Coal distributed by private contribution	60

EDWARD L. CORNER, President   ALFRED CANNON, Vice-President

JAMES R. ANDERSON, Treasurer   LOUIS D. CASNER, Secretary

Reports for 1928 and 1931, showing the Soup Society's distribution before the stock market crash and after in 1931, once the Depression started. *Kensington Soup Society Archives.*

The Pennsylvania Sugar Company, at Shackamaxon Street and Delaware Avenue, was a neighborhood institution. During economic downturns, sugarhouse workers were helped by the Soup Society, 1914.

KENSINGTON SOUP SOCIETY

Chartered April 18th, 1853   1036 CREASE STREET

Philadelphia, April 5, 1930.

The Kensington Soup Society appeals to the charitably inclined for support of this Institution to carry on its work for the coming winter.

Contributions for the work of the Society are needed and will be appreciated.

Donations, Checks or Money may be sent to the Society in care of the Treasurer, Mr. James R. Anderson, 1135 Shackamaxon Street.

Summary of the operation of the Society for the winter Dec. 16, 1929, to April 5, 1930:

No. of Loaves of Bread distributed	16,402
No. of Pints of Soup distributed	77,080
No. of Families supplied	115
Average No. of Families supplied	85
No. of Half Tons of Coal distributed by private contribution	45

EDWARD L. CORNER, President   ALFRED CANNON, Vice-President

JAMES R. ANDERSON, Treasurer   LOUIS D. CASNER, Secretary

KENSINGTON SOUP SOCIETY

Chartered April 18th, 1853   1036 CREASE STREET

Philadelphia, January 1st, 1935.

The Kensington Soup Society appeals to the charitably inclined for support of this Institution to carry on its work for the coming winter.

Contributions for the work of the Society are needed and will be appreciated.

Donations, Checks or Money may be sent to the Society in care of the Treasurer, Mr. James R. Anderson, 1135 Shackamaxon Street.

Summary of the operation of the Society for the winter Jan. 2, 1934 to March 24, 1934

No. of Loaves of Bread distributed	9100
No. of Pints of Soup distributed	71,680
No. of Families supplied	305
Average No. of Families supplied	105
No. of $\frac{1}{2}$ Tons of Coal distributed by private contribution	20
Free Bowls of Soup (and Bread) to Needy Men	3136

EDWARD L. CORNER, President   ALFRED CANNON Vice-President

JAMES R. ANDERSON, Treasurer   HAROLD TITHER, Secretary

Summary reports for the years 1930 and 1935, showing the Soup Society's distribution during the Great Depression. *Kensington Soup Society Archives.*

greatly exceeded the previous year and increased again the following year before decreasing for the next several years, rising slightly during the brief recession of 1937. The decade of the 1930s was the worst of times for local residents and the Soup Society was there when it was needed to help get the neighborhood through the Depression.

Not only did the Depression create increased demands on the available Soup Society resources, it also soon outstripped the potential donor base, since the Depression also hit those wealthy benefactors who had traditionally donated to the society. At one point in April 1933, the Soup Society's treasury had on hand only $10.43, with bills amounting to over $770.00. While the Soup Society did have financial investments it could have drawn on, that would have necessitated selling off interest-bearing bonds, securities or mortgages, which would mean losing future revenues from interest-bearing investments. Instead, the society decided to borrow $1,000 from vice-president and superintendent Alfred Cannon to cover current expenses rather than diminish its long-term investments. Cannon had previously loaned the Soup Society $1,500 in 1931.

It was not until 1937, six years after securing its first loan from Cannon, that the Soup Society would be in a financial position to repay him for both loans, and even then, only after receiving over $17,000 from the estate of George Thomas in 1935. Truly, the Soup Society's abilities were stretched to their limits during the Great Depression.

TABLE 6: Kensington Soup Society's distribution statistics for the decade of the Great Depression.

Year	Soup (gals)	Bread (lvs)	Families (per)	Persons (daily)	Coal (tns)
1929–30	7,200	10,508	90 (6 per)	125	25
1930–31	10,402	9,635	115(6 per)	85 (families)	30
1931–32	14,633	23,499	298	155 (families)	30
1932–33	11,793	18,533	229	155 (families)	24.5
1933–34	11,615	21,504	297 (5 per)	200 (families)	19
1934–35	8,960	9,100	205 (6 per)	105 (families)	10
1935–36	5,620	4,412	83	45	11.5
1936–37	6,665	6,669	122	80	18
1937–38	6,320	6,073	117	70	12.5
1938–39	7,490	9,292	150		22.75

Soup (gals) = gallons of soup; Bread (lvs) = loaves of bread; Families (per) = persons per family; Persons (daily) = persons daily; Coal (tns) = tons of coal in half-ton deliveries per house.

From the statistics shown above in Table 6, we can see how as the years went on the amount of charity dispensed grew, until the economy started to right itself and the need decreased.

At about this time, at a meeting in December 1938, the Board of Managers ordered the secretary to secure "Liability & Compensation Insurance on both the help and Real Estate owned by the Soup House." This is the first mention of securing insurance on the property or workers in the Soup Society's history.

WORLD WAR II, 1940–1945

Edward L. Corner was still president of the Kensington Soup Society at the outbreak of World War II. The Soup Society needed to meet the increased demands and changing needs of local residents, since many husbands and fathers were being called up for war, leaving their wives and children to seek other means of support during their absence. Since a number of relief programs had been set up in the 1930s, the Soup Society did not have to meet the community's demands all by itself, as it had previously had to do.

The first few years of the fighting (1939–41) saw America caught between official neutrality and unofficial support to its allies. However, by late 1941 America had entered the war, and the statistics for the Soup House reflected the new demands for charity increasing that year (see Table 7 below). These levels remained high for two years running before dropping even further than prewar levels.

TABLE 7: Charity distributed by the Kensington Soup Society during the era of World War II, 1940–45.

Year	Soup (gals)	Bread (lvs)	Families (per)	Persons	Coal (tns)
1939–40	6,420	6,640	85 (5 per)		24.5
1940–41	6,868	9,715	86 (5 per)		27
1941–42	7,510	5,995	138 (5 per)		20
1942–43	4,051	5,617	130	3,914	17
1943–44	2,615	2,314	43 (5 per)		21
1944–45	3,055	1,886	42 (5 per)		17

Kensington Soup Society
OF PHILADELPHIA
No. 1036 Crease Street

No.

Name _____

Residence _____

is entitled to_____pints of Soup.

For the }
Committee. }

Philad'a,   Mo.   194

M	T	W	T	F	S	M	T	W	T	F	S
13						14					
11						12					
9						10					
7						8					
5						6					
3						4					
1						2					

Circa 1940s "entitlement card," which, after completed by the Soup Society, allowed the bearer to receive soup at the Soup House. *Kensington Soup Society Archives.*

In response to the war effort, the Soup Society invested money in defense bonds and victory loan offers. In 1942, the society invested $2,500 at 2½ percent in victory loans and another $2,500 in defense bonds, Series G (also at 2½ percent). At this time, the Soup Society had almost $22,000 on deposit at the Kensington National Bank. The next year (1943), the Soup Society invested $10,000 in the fourth war loan government bonds at 2½ percent interest. When the sixth war loan was offered, the Soup Society invested another $10,000 in 1944, also at 2½ percent interest.

The Soup Society also invested in the Penn Treaty Building Association by investing $2,500 in 1942 and the same amount in 1943. The full stock paid 4 percent interest. Again in 1951 and twice in 1952, the Soup Society made further investments in the Penn Treaty Building Association, for a total investment of at least $20,000 between 1942 and 1952. It was investing money in the East Girard Avenue Building Association as well. Who better to know the success of these building associations than the Soup Society, since in the 1840s, the society's Board of Managers had founded the Kensington Building Association, the most successful building association in America's history and the model for all later building associations.

With the end of World War II in 1945, the American economy began one of its biggest expansions in history, as the United States helped to rebuild the various countries devastated during the war. As might be expected, as the economy improved, the need decreased for the services of organizations such as the Kensington Soup Society. However, the immediate post–World War II statistics (see Table 8 below) of the Soup House would not appear to bear this out, since the number of individuals and families that needed charity was still fairly large. This need for charity may have been the result of a number of factors: men returning from war who were wounded, maimed or crippled; families that never recovered from the loss of income during the war years; displaced persons due to the war; persons out of work as war contracts dried up; or the postwar recession.

TABLE 8: Distribution statistics for the Kensington Soup Society for the seven years immediately following the end of World War II.

Year	Soup (gals)	Bread (lvs)	Families	Persons	Coal (tns)
1945–46*	1,810	695	26	846	16
1946–47**					
1947–48	1,935	1,294	46	6,824	44
1948–49	2,257	1,536	60	8,328	36
1949–50	2,535	1,673	60	9,221	28
1950–51	3,110	1,694	178	9,733	23
1951–52	2,839	1,396	178	8,132	26

*Statistics for these years are incomplete
**Soup House was closed for this year

THE 100TH ANNIVERSARY OF THE KENSINGTON SOUP SOCIETY, 1944

At the Annual Contributors Meeting held on December 2, 1943, Edward L. Corner was elected to his twenty-fourth year as the president of the Kensington Soup Society, the longest running presidency up to that time. However, Corner's twenty-fourth anniversary as president would be upstaged by the planning for the society's own celebration of its 100th anniversary. At the managers meeting that followed the contributors meeting in December 1943, President Corner appointed Vice-president Walter Gilman as the chairman of the 100th Anniversary Committee. On the committee with Gilman were President Corner, Superintendent John Radcliffe, Treasurer

James R. Anderson, Secretary Harold Tither and Board of Managers member T. Ridge Yerkes.

At the next Board of Managers meeting held on February 10, 1944, the 100th Anniversary Committee (with approval from the Board of Managers) stated that it would hold "a banquet and have a booklet printed to celebrate our 100th anniversary, the cost of which is to be paid by the Soup Society." At the next meeting of the Board of Managers, held on April 19, 1944, the minutes reported that "progress" was being made on the "Anniversary Program."

After the Annual Contributors Meeting that was held on December 15, 1944, the Board of Managers convened and President Edward L. Corner reported "progress in making arrangements for Anniversary program." While Corner might have thought progress was actually being made in planning the event, there was a storm brewing over the event, since some on the Board of Managers were opposed to it.

The main person who objected to the banquet and the only one for which actual evidence exists is Walter Gilman, the vice-president of the Soup Society as well as the chairman of the 100th Anniversary Committee. Gilman, in a letter dated December 19, 1944, and sent to President Corner, stated that there were "other active members of the Society [who] are of the same opinion."

Gilman first joined the Board of Managers of the Soup Society in 1915 as one of the auxiliary managers, in which position he served until 1921, when he became a full manager. In 1935, he was elected to the vice-presidency of the society and held that position until 1950. He took an active interest in the Soup House on the House Committee from 1921 to 1950, and while not stated, he presumably would have been the chairman of that committee, since he was its oldest member. The House Committee, in conjunction with the steward and superintendent, was the main group of managers that ran the everyday activities of the Soup House.

Walter Gilman was born in Kensington about 1876. He grew up in the neighborhood of Front and Otter (Wildey) Streets. His father appears to have been William Gilman, probably the son of Ambrose Gilman. Both William and Ambrose worked as boilermakers. Ambrose was a partner in the firm of Ambrose & Farran, at Front and Wildey. William took over the family business and, by at least 1890, moved it to the 1100 block of Beach Street, while he moved to 1110 Frankford Avenue.

Walter Gilman, growing up in a family of machinists and boilermakers, first worked as a civil engineer before moving into the mining field. He

The laying of the cornerstone of the Edward Corner building, Shackamaxon Street and Delaware Avenue, 1921. *Courtesy of Jeanne Robson, an Edward Corner descendant.*

worked as a mining engineer for many years, was successful and eventually became a partner in a firm. He lived for a number of years on the 1300 block of East Susquehanna Avenue, before moving to Castor and Allengrove, in the Northwood section of Frankford.

President Corner appointed Gilman to the chairmanship of the 100th Anniversary Committee. One would think that, as chairman, Gilman would have guided the flow of conversation for the planning of the 100th anniversary, but as Gilman's letter shows (printed on the next page), that would not be the case.

Gilman and Corner were old friends. Corner, like Gilman, was one of the longest serving members of the Board of Managers, having first been elected in 1906. The year 1944 was his thirty-eighth in service to the Soup Society. Except for the treasurer, James R. Anderson, who was first elected to the position in 1914 and had been on the Board of Managers since 1910, the other officers were all comparative newcomers in relation to Anderson, Corner and Gilman. Secretary Harold Tither and

Superintendent John Radcliffe had been elected to their positions nine years previously in 1935. The only other person on the 100th Anniversary Committee was Board of Managers member T. Ridge Yerkes, who had recently joined the board in 1942.

But for the survival of Walter Gilman's letter to Edward L. Corner, this chapter of the Soup Society's history may have gone unnoticed. Gilman's reasoning for being set against the anniversary banquet is rather interesting when one thinks of today's charitable organizations and the "sumptuous" banquets they hold for themselves with their donors' monies. For this reason, Gilman's letter deserves to be printed verbatim:

Mr. Edward L. Corner, President
Kensington Soup Society
1210 E. Columbia Ave.,
Philadelphia, (25) Penna.

Dear Ed,

Since the meeting of the Kensington Soup Society last Friday night I have given considerable thought to the proposed celebration of the 100th anniversary of the founding of the organization. I intended phoning you regarding the matter but finally decided to write and thereby avoid any misunderstanding.

As you undoubtedly know I have never favored the banquet part of the celebration and am still strongly of the opinion that a banquet is not appropriate for a charitable organization like the Kensington Soup Society. Rather than benefit the organization it may be productive of harmful results. A sumptuous banquet, for the present officers of the Society and their friends, does not seem to harmonize with a bowl of soup and a half-loaf of bread for the unfortunate through funds given for that particular purpose and not for celebrations.

It was my understanding the proposed banquet was for the sole purpose of honoring those who in the past were instrumental in obtaining the necessary funds to keep the Society in operation. According to the plan presented last Friday night this does not seem to be the object as no mention was made of the Thomas', Williamson's and others who bequeathed considerable money to the Society to perpetuate its existence. The objective appeared to be the glorification of the present officers through full-page portraits in the menu-booklet.

Instead of a banquet the distribution of a booklet, reciting the history of the Society and its accomplishments during the last 100 years and giving full credit to all who have made it possible either through personal interest or gifts would, I think, be more appropriate for the 100th anniversary and would form an indelible record for the future.

Personally, I am so opposed to a banquet that I do not care to have anything to do with this part of the program and, if given, will not be present. In fact, I must request that you eliminate my name from the committee, which, up to the present time has only been a committee in name at any rate. This does not mean that I will offer any opposition to the banquet, which was authorized, at one of the Society's meetings. I merely want to record that fact that I do not approve of it and believe some of the other active members of the Society are of the same opinion.

Sincerely yours,
Walter Gilman

After Gilman sent his letter to Corner, there is not another mention of the anniversary banquet until the February 1945 meeting of the Board of Managers. At that meeting, President Corner made a general report on the anniversary booklet that was being put together. This was the last time the anniversary banquet was mentioned in the monthly minutes of the Board of Managers meetings. In addition, the archives of the Soup Society do not show any other mention of the anniversary banquet or booklet after this February 1945 date. There is also no mention in the treasurer's reports that money was ever spent between 1943 and 1946 on the anniversary banquet or the booklet.

It is unclear why the anniversary banquet or booklet was never mentioned again. It is also unclear if the anniversary banquet ever took place or if the booklet was ever printed. There is also no evidence that a one-hundred-year history of the Soup Society was ever written, as suggested by Gilman. No anniversary booklet or history exists in the Soup Society's archives; thus, we are left to wonder and make presumptions on what happened. Did Gilman's letter to Corner put an end to it all?

The Soup Society's archive contains a mockup of the planned booklet, presumably put together by a member or members of the 100th Anniversary Committee. The booklet was to include full-page portraits of the Soup Society's officers, apparently one of the major objections by Gilman. It could be that there was some sort of celebration, perhaps scaled down, but the only evidence that remains are papers from the planning stages of the event and not from the actual event itself. The available evidence would seem to suggest that in the end, Walter Gilman and those aligned with his thinking may have won out, or at least forced the Soup Society to have a more low-key event.

While it is unclear if the Soup Society ever did have its anniversary banquet, there are some documents that survived that give insights into what the 100th Anniversary Committee had hoped that the affair would be. During its days planning the celebration, the committee formed a list of the previous benefactors whom they wanted to make known to the gathered supporters of the society. This list was to be included in the anniversary booklet that would be published for the event. The list of the honored past benefactors and/or managers of the society was four pages long and included seventy-eight individuals, thirty-two businesses, six estates and five churches. Many of the individuals were previous officers of the Soup Society or members of the Board of Managers. These individuals and churches, as well as the businesses that were listed, read like a who's who of Kensington for the last half of the nineteenth century and the beginning decades of the twentieth.

Former congressman and Soup Society president, the Honorable John Robbins, was listed, as were local businessmen Alpheus Wilt, Henry Disston and Edwin F. Fitler (who had become mayor of Philadelphia). These were men who started their businesses in Kensington or were born in Kensington, and they created companies that were some of the best in the country in their respective fields. Disston, in particular, regularly gave the Soup Society $50 or $100 during the annual collections. People like financier A.J. Drexel were also listed as previous backers of the Soup Society, often contributing $50 to the society during the annual collections. These were just a few of the seventy-eight individuals honored on the list as having been supporters of the Soup Society in the past.

Two local banks were mentioned on the past benefactors list: the Kensington National Bank, the bank of the Soup Society and a bank whose Board of Directors partially overlapped with the Soup Society over the years; and the Eighth National Bank, which was formerly located at Second Street and Girard Avenue and was controlled by Kensington businessmen.

Since Kensington had been a shipbuilding community, it was not surprising to see shipbuilders Birely, Hillman, & Streaker, Neafie & Levy and the famed William Cramp & Sons on the list as previous benefactors. Frankford Avenue's hosiery giant, the Martin Landenberger Company, was also mentioned. Other companies like the Philadelphia & Reading Rail

Road, the rolling mills of James Rowland & Sons and lumber merchant Alexander Adaire's company, Adaire & Mullica, were all included in the list of thirty-two businesses honored as having supported the Soup Society during its one-hundred-year history. There were obviously many more, but only the main ones tended to be listed.

The six estates on the list that had set up legacies to support the Soup Society were the A.R. Chambers, Jeanes, Henry Kessler, George W. Jesse, George S. Pepper and Sepviva Estates. These estates permitted steady financing to the Soup Society over the years. For example, in December 1899, the Pepper Estate paid a dividend of $150 and a distribution of income of $275 in 1903, this on income ($5,000) originally given back in 1890 when Pepper died. At least as early as the 1870s and into the twentieth century, the Chambers Estate appears to have been paying a small yearly dividend to the Soup Society.

There were many more bequests, in particular the bequest of over $17,000 by the will of Charles G. Thomas in 1936, which helped eliminate debt during the Depression, and the monies donated by John D. Williamson that set up the Williamson Coal Fund, which allowed the Soup Society yearly donations for delivering coal to the needy. When Soup Society president Alexander H. McFadden died in 1900, his estate contributed at least $2,850 to the Soup Society.

The churches listed as benefactors were the five Protestant churches that had always been there to help support the operations of the Kensington Soup Society: Kensington Methodist Episcopal, First Presbyterian of Kensington, East Baptist, Pilgrim Congregational and, later, Siloam Methodist Episcopal. These churches took up an annual collection called the Union Thanksgiving Collection. The collection was taken around the Thanksgiving holiday and given to the Soup Society, where it was generally reported in the Annual Contributors Meeting the first week of December. In 1917, the amount of monies collected by the churches was $43.33 and in 1919, only $33.46, but the following year it was $50.00. The collection taken for Thanksgiving by Reverend Woolston's East Baptist Church in 1924 amounted to $63.60, while in 1926, Pilgrim Congregational Church alone gave the Soup Society $50.82. In 1928, the total collection amounted to $48.92. The collections appear to average about $50.00 annually during the 1920s. By the 1940s, these collections were upward of $100.00 per year.

This Union Thanksgiving Collection started as early as the 1870s, if not earlier, and continued until 1954, at which time the Board of Managers of the Soup Society, in a letter written by newly elected president James

World War I, the Great Depression and World War II

First Presbyterian Church of Kensington, Girard Avenue, north of Columbia Avenue. This local church ran fundraisers for the Soup Society.

First Presbyterian Church today, minus the steeple, which had to be removed after a storm in the early decades of the twentieth century.

R. Anderson Jr., felt that to honor the passing of their longtime president, Edward L. Corner, the respective churches should continue to make the collection, but the host church should keep the monies and use it toward something that it might see proper. This is also an indication that the Kensington Soup Society finances were sound, after a period of liquidating its real estate investments and investing the monies in building associations and the stock market. In addition, the needs of the community were not as great as they had been, particularly as a result of the various federal government subsidy programs that came about with the arrival of the federal assistance programs in America in the 1930s.

There has also survived a list of individuals invited to attend the 100th anniversary celebration. The list includes 92 individuals invited by the Soup Society's Board of Managers, with an additional 23 guests (perhaps friends and family of those invited), for a total of 115 people. At the top of the list was a former Republican mayor of Philadelphia, W. Freeland Kendrick, as well as the Democratic opponent he defeated in the 1924 election, the Honorable A. Raymond Raff. Besides members of the Soup Society's Board of Managers, their wives and families, the invited guests also included the ministers and Boards of Trustees of the local supportive churches. For example, the Board of Trustees of East Baptist Church was invited, which included Soup Society Board of Managers member T. Ridge Yerkes and Superintendent John Radcliffe.

Those with previous ties to the Soup Society were also invited, such as the widows of former board members and officers, people like Mrs. Alexander H. McFadden, the wife of the former president of the society. Other relatives of former officers were invited, like Annie Smeeton, who was related to Samuel and Thomas Smeeton, who served on the Board of Managers; Samuel was also president from 1901 to 1908. Members of the Williamson family were also invited, as the family had given so generously to the Soup Society, particularly in establishing the Williamson Coal Fund.

From what little evidence remains, it would appear that the banquet was planned to be held at a local church, presumably Kensington Methodist Episcopal, as that is the church that the Soup Society had the strongest relationship with over the years. The 115 attendees were to be treated to a banquet to be catered by D.F. McCallister & Sons especially to a Soup House crowd. The menu included a choice of soups, including stewed snapper a la McCallister, snapper soup and pepper pot, as well as hard rolls, ice cream and ices, fancy cakes and coffee. The buffet-style serving would cost the Soup Society $1.15 per person.

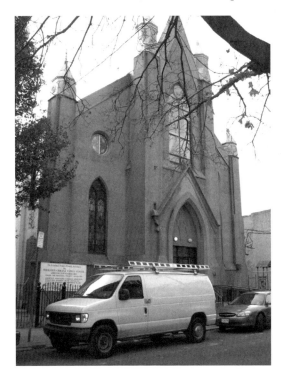

East Baptist Church, Columbia Avenue, west of Girard Avenue, is now closed. The church regularly collected a Union Thanksgiving Collection for the Soup Society.

Penn Widows' Asylum, Belgrade Street and Susquehanna Avenue. It had several boards of directors that overlapped with the Soup Society.

While the banquet menu does not sound as "sumptuous" as Walter Gilman stated in his letter to Corner, it could be that the menu was revised due to Gilman's objections.

THE DEATH OF LONGTIME STEWARD CHRISTIAN SCHERZ

While the 100th Anniversary Committee was busy planning the banquet, a major disruption occurred that would affect the Soup Society for some time. The Soup Society's longtime steward, Christian Scherz, died at the age of sixty-seven. Scherz had first been appointed to the steward position in 1915 and served for thirty years continuously in that position. It was the most years served by a steward in the society's one-hundred-year history. His wife, Suzie Scherz, had served alongside her husband as assistant steward for all that time. The couple had lived and worked at the Soup House on Crease Street since Christian became the steward. Suzie was a German immigrant, having only come to America in 1906. Christian Scherz was the son of a German immigrant. His father, Henri Scherz, was a weaver who lived on the 1100 block of Howard Street, near Girard. Before moving into the Soup House, Christian worked as a tin roofer and lived with his wife at his father's home. The couple does not appear to have had any children; thus, they were able to devote thirty years of their lives to the mission of the Kensington Soup Society.

While it was indeed a very sad day for the Soup Society, its members paid their respects to Christian Scherz with the following resolution that was adopted and recorded in the minutes of the April 1945 Soup Society meeting ledger:

> *Whereas we learn with deep sorrow of the death of our friend and associate, our faithful and devoted steward Christian J. Scherz and desire to express our appreciation of his devoted service to the work he gave so many years of his life, Therefore be it resolved that we place on our minutes a record of our appreciation of his splendid loyalty, his unblemished Christian character, his unselfishness and love for humanity, whose heart was always open to the call and needs of the poor and destitute whom he delighted to help and whom it was his pleasure to relieve, and among whom he worked, and our sense of great loss in his removal from our midst, and our deep sympathy for the loss sustained by his wife, Suzie Scherz.*

CLOSING OF THE SOUP HOUSE FOR THE SEASON OF 1945–46

As if the problems over the anniversary banquet and the death of the longtime steward were not enough, the Soup Society faced another difficulty. For the first time in the one-hundred-year recorded history of the Kensington Soup Society, the Soup House was forced to close for a season. The Soup Society had difficulty finding another suitable steward. After Christian Scherz's thirty years on the job, it would appear that the Board of Managers was stymied to find someone to replace such a dedicated person. The job was offered to Suzie Scherz, but she declined to stay on at the Soup House after the death of her husband.

By December 1945, when the Soup House should have been getting ready to open for the 1945–46 season, John Radcliffe, who had been the superintendent since 1939, abruptly resigned. While the Board of Managers regretted his resignation, they accepted it nonetheless. Although the board received plenty of applications for the steward position, none of the applicants was found suitable by the board. Thus, without a steward or a superintendent, the board decided to close the Soup House for the season of 1945–46. The Williamson Coal Fund was still distributed to the needy in the neighborhood and the borders of the Soup Society's distribution area were expanded. Now residents in that area between Frankford Avenue and Richmond Street, and up as far north as Lehigh Avenue, were eligible for the charity of the Soup House.

The Soup Society reopened its doors the very next season, after the hiring of Thomas Stafford as the superintendent. The society also received word from Suzie Scherz that she would come back and serve as the stewardess for the coming season (1946–47), provided satisfactory arrangements could be made. Apparently the closing of the Soup House for the previous year was enough of a shock for Mrs. Scherz to make her change her mind. As a bonus for opening up after being closed for the year, the Soup Society had the Soup House painted inside and out.

CHAPTER 8

CHANGING SHAPES OF THE KENSINGTON SOUP SOCIETY

THE CHANGING OF THE OLD GUARD, 1945–1955

For the thirty-year period from 1915 to 1945, a period when America went through World War I, the Great Depression and World War II, the Soup Society was fortunate to have a core group of managers and officers to help guide it through some of the hardest times in its history. During this time there were thirteen individuals who served continuously for decades at a time, which helped the Soup Society to have a full 50 to 75 percent of its Board of Managers unchanged during this period. That core group of thirteen were: James R. Anderson, 1910–45; Alfred Cannon, 1917–39; Edward L. Corner, 1906–45; Alan Cowdrick, 1911–45; Charles L. Cushmore, 1908–45; Walter Gilman, 1915–45; Godfrey C. Rebmann, 1908–45; H.S. Rebmann, 1908–45; William F. Sauter, 1911–45; Christian Scherz, 1915–45; Suzie Scherz, 1915–45; John B. Tuttle, 1918–42; and John D. Williamson Jr., 1911–42.

The decade of the 1940s saw the old guard of the Soup Society dying off, retiring or being replaced. First it was Alfred Cannon leaving before the war started in 1939, and then John B. Tuttle died in 1942. The year 1942 also saw the last member of the Williamson family leave the Soup Society, John D. Williamson Jr. In April 1945, the Soup Society saw the death of longtime steward Christian Scherz, which forced his wife Suzie to temporarily leave as stewardess. She came back after the year the Soup Society closed but then finally retired in 1953. In a letter written to President Edward L. Corner, Mrs. Scherz stated the following:

David S. Clunn, a Girard Avenue stationer, served thirty-two years either on the Board of Managers or as advisory manager for the Soup Society.

I wish to thank you, Mrs. Corner and everyone connected with the Kensington Soup Society for your kindness to me for these many years. But now the time has come when I no longer will be able to do this work so will you kindly accept this as my resignation as Stewardess of the Kensington Soup Society.

It grieves me deeply to disassociate myself from your organization, but I am acting upon my doctor's orders.

With that, Suzie Scherz ended her thirty-eight-year relationship with the Soup Society as its stewardess, the longest in the Soup House's history.

Other old guard members like Charles L. Cushmore were gone from the board by 1948. Treasurer James R. Anderson died in 1949 and when his son, James R. Anderson Jr., tried to secure his father's treasurer position, T. Ridge Yerkes defeated him in the elections of 1949, one of the very few contested elections in the Soup Society's then 105-year history. Less then two months after the junior Anderson lost the election for treasurer, Vice-president Walter Gilman resigned in February 1950. Whether the contested election that had the son of an old guard manager being defeated had anything to do with Gilman's resignation is not known. However, eight of the thirteen old guard members were gone by 1950, and a new era of the

The burial plot of the Soup Society's George Kessler is located at Palmer Cemetery. After Laurel Hill Cemetery, Palmer Cemetery claims many early founders.

Soup Society's history was entered. The loss of the old guard had dramatic effects on the Soup Society and its operations.

Five new members joined the Board of Managers in the auxiliary manager positions in 1942. They were: James R. Anderson Jr., Everett G Mourer, Clarence B. Hackman, T. Ridge Yerkes and John Phipps. These five men, along with those who were elected in the 1930s (John Radcliffe, Harold Tither and William Rowan Grant), were the new generation that would help to usher the Soup Society into its second century.

RESTRUCTURING THE FINANCES AND MISSION OF THE SOUP SOCIETY

While it is unclear if the Soup Society had a Finance Committee all along, the committee was first mentioned in the regular monthly meeting minutes of 1948. It could have been the brainchild of the new treasurer, T. Ridge Yerkes, who became treasurer in 1949 but had been on the Board of

Managers since 1942 and had been helping the aging and sickly longtime treasurer, James R. Anderson. When Anderson died, Yerkes beat out Anderson's son, James Jr., in one of the few contested elections in the Soup Society's long history. However, Anderson Jr. soon became vice-president in 1952 and then president of the Soup Society in 1955 upon the death of Edward L. Corner.

In all probability, the duties of the Finance Committee were taken care of by the House and Real Estate Committee, in conjunction with the treasurer. In an attempt to modernize and streamline the Soup Society's financial matters, the Finance Committee was created out of the House and Real Estate Committee, splitting its duties with the House Committee, focusing on taking care of the Soup House while the new Finance Committee took care of the real estate and other investments. Coincidentally or not, it was in 1948 that the process of selling off the real estate holdings of the Soup Society started.

In order to make the above-mentioned investments in the building associations, the Soup Society began a strategy of liquidating real estate holdings during the period from 1948 to 1958. In conjunction with the city of Philadelphia reaching its peak population in 1950 and the surge in government-backed GI home mortgage loans for returning soldiers from World War II, it was a good time to divest of real estate and put the monies to work in the building and loan sector.

Typical block of red brick row houses along Rosehill Street. The Soup Society invested in developments like this, cashing out in the 1950s.

Between the years 1948 and 1958, the Soup Society sold the following properties:

2512 East Norris Street (sold the ground rent interest) $60/yearly, sold in 1948

⅛ share of 35 lots in fortieth ward, $100, sold in 1950

1435 North Orkney for $500, sold in 1951

6634 Haddington Street for $5,000, sold in 1952

6731 North Marsden Street, forty-first ward, for $5,500, sold in 1952

1028 West Master Street for $1,800, sold in 1953

1612 North Hope Street for $1,600, sold in 1953

5728 Rodman Street for $5,200, sold in 1953

6373 North Marsden Street for $5,500, sold in 1953

3215 Arlington Street, thirty-second ward, for $4,800, sold in 1954

6111 Hegerman Street, forty-first ward, for $5,000, sold in 1956

The selling off of these properties brought $34,500 to the coffers of the Soup Society. The Finance Committee decided to invest some of the money raised in the purchase of eighty-eight shares of AT&T stock at $165 per share, as well as the previously mentioned investments in the building associations. Also, in late 1954, the Soup Society invested $10,000 in the Wellington Trust Fund.

In 1955, the Soup Society saw the death of its longtime president, Edward L. Corner. Corner had been a member of the Board of Managers since 1906 and president since 1919. The very next year, the Soup Society saw two successive deaths among the Board of Managers—Harold Tithers, secretary, and John Phipps, a member of the Board of Managers. John Radcliffe, who had previously retired in 1952, also died that year. Thus, the Board of Managers for the November 29, 1956 Annual Contributors Meeting consisted of only James R. Anderson Jr., George E. Williams, T. Ridge Yerkes and John E. Slack. There was no mention of the election of auxiliary managers for the seasons of 1955–56 or 1956–57. These positions had been in existence since the 1911–12 season, when the Board of Managers was split in half, with half becoming the actual managers and the other half being able to participate in the proceedings of the board. It is unclear why the Soup Society eliminated the auxiliary managers; perhaps their function had been outlived and there was no further need for them as managers of the Soup Society. In addition, hired help provided all the manpower that was needed for the operations of the Soup Society, which

Edward Corner served on the Board of Managers of the Soup Society for forty-nine years (1906–55), thirty-six of those years as president; he was the longest reigning president. *Kensington Soup Society Archives.*

were shrinking. With the elimination of the auxiliary managers and the death of Edward L. Corner, the Soup Society lost the last of the remaining old guard mentioned previously: Edward Corner, Allen Cowdrick, William F. Sauter, H.F. Rebmann and Godfrey C. Rebmann.

The changes and downsizing of the Soup Society reflected what was occurring overall in American society. The advent of federal and local welfare programs reduced local residents' dependence on the Soup House. Even the Williamson Coal Fund was affected by the growth of welfare. Charles F. Weeks reported in a House Committee Report of April 4, 1963, that the Soup House had delivered no coal and that residents were registering at the Department of Public Assistance to receive coal deliveries.

As other soup houses began closing, the Kensington Soup Society expanded its borders in 1945 in an attempt to draw in more people. Later in 1955, the Soup House, prompted by Vice-president George E. Williams, examined its bylaws to see if it might be able to "extend [its] Charity to other needy organizations." The first duty of incoming president James R. Anderson Jr. after the death of Edward L. Corner in 1955 was to notify the various local church pastors that it was no longer necessary to take up the

The East Columbia Avenue home of longtime Soup Society president Edward Corner, a local businessman and philanthropist. *Kensington Soup Society Archives.*

Union Thanksgiving Collection, taken up every year since at least the 1870s on behalf of the Soup Society. This would appear to be one of the first signs that the services of the Soup House were now in decline and that the society was thinking of redirecting its funds and investments toward other charitable possibilities.

The Soup Society experienced a number of changes during the 1940s and 1950s. First there was the dispute between William Gilman and Edward Corner over the 100th anniversary celebration and how it should be celebrated. Secondly, the old guard died off, resulting in the contested election when T. Ridge Yerkes defeated James R. Anderson Jr. for control of the accounts of the Soup Society. Third, with the changing of the treasurer and the removal of the old guard, the control of the finances and policy involved changed from real estate investments to divesting real estate and reinvesting in building associations, the stock market and trust funds. Finally, the Board of Managers eliminated the auxiliary managers, thus reducing the board from a high of twenty-three in 1925 to eighteen in 1935, then sixteen in 1945 and finally only seven in 1955, when the auxiliary Board of Managers was eliminated.

THE FORGOTTEN YEARS, 1959–1981

Unfortunately, the archives of the Soup Society do not contain the monthly meeting minutes for the period from 1959 to 1981, a full twenty-two years. Thus, we cannot determine how the new developments affected the Soup Society but only speculate after examining a comparison of before and after. Some correspondence exists, which helps to identify some of the officers and managers of the Soup Society during this period, in addition to a stack of cancelled checks from December 1957 to September 1962. We can see, therefore, what vendors were being paid, as well as staff and board members. Oddly enough, even the financial records and the gas, electric and telephone bills for this period are missing. It is as if a box or two of material was simply lost, misplaced or destroyed for some reason.

One of the last tasks that the new Board of Managers carried out at a meeting in May 1957 (before the records are mute for the next twenty-two years) was to vote its members a salary for carrying out their duties as officers of the Soup Society—duties that had been voluntary since 1844. This may

Looking westward at the 1000 block of Crease Street, the Soup House's façade still looks good after 138 years.

or may not show the new policy of the Board of Managers, or it may reflect their economic status in life. The board was no longer composed of men of wealth doing their duty as good Christians, but employees expecting compensation for their charitable work.

At this May 1957 meeting, a recommendation was made that the secretary's position be combined with the treasurer's position but President James R. Anderson Jr. did not consider that a good idea, so the positions remained separate. Soon after this motion was made, Anderson resigned his position as president and offered to take over as permanent secretary, which the board accepted. Anderson then nominated George E. Williams to take over as president, which the board agreed to. The salaries were then set for the officers, with Anderson's new position being the most remunerative, $400 per year, or about $3,000 in today's money. The president's position paid $200 per year, the treasurer $300 and the vice-president $100. Anderson thus steered the board away from combining the secretary and treasurer positions and took the top paying position for himself. The salaries were also made retroactive to the last meeting.

Without the monthly meeting minute ledgers, the Soup Society history lacks a record of its activities from 1959 to 1981; however, assorted correspondence exists among the officers of the Soup Society. One such letter, dated May 19, 1965, and addressed to H.N. Nash & Co., states: "Be advised that the following officers were duly elected on May 9, 1957 on a permanent basis or until they were succeeded. President—George E. Williams, Secretary—James R. Anderson, Jr., Treasurer—T. Ridge Yerkes."

This letter would seem to indicate that there was no longer an Annual Contributors Meeting at which nominations were taken and the Board of Managers elected. The meeting of 1957 created a Board of Managers that was self-perpetuating and not elected. However, a reading of the minutes at that May 1957 meeting does not indicate that any of the officers were to hold their positions until their replacement or demise.

Why this sudden change took place in 1957, wherein the Board of Managers would not continue to be elected, is unclear. Upon the death of longtime president Edward L. Corner, the last of the old guard had departed and their counterparts among the new generation saw fit to govern the Soup Society differently. Perhaps, as we have already seen, the mission of the Soup Society was becoming less relevant or needed in the community. While individuals and families still showed up to accept charity, there were many alternatives available through federal, state and municipal government agencies, and more often than not, if something is given freely, there will always be takers. Thus, people will always show up regardless if there is an actual need or not.

The change in the Board of Managers election procedure may be due to the fact that many of the Protestants who had dominated the Fishtown and Kensington communities for so long were now dying out or moving away, and consequently the small Protestant churches were also closing their doors. It was from this Protestant population that the Soup Society generally elected the men who had governed the society for so long. The area had become predominantly Roman Catholic in the twentieth century, and perhaps as a way to maintain the Protestant control of the Soup Society (which it had always been), the board was transformed from freely elected to self-perpetuating. This, of course, is only a theory and is difficult to prove one way or the other, due to the missing records for this period.

Based on the May 19, 1965 letter and from others that exist, we do know that Superintendent John E. Slack resigned in November 1958 due to health reasons and that James R. Anderson Jr. continued as secretary until at least May 1965. T. Ridge Yerkes was still the treasurer in November 1965. In addition, George E. Williams was presumably still the president in May 1965. Amanda Schenkel appears to have continued on as stewardess until at least April 1959. It also looks like the Soup Society may have hired an individual by the name of Charles F. Weeks as the possible superintendent during the seasons of 1961–63. Weeks was followed by Charles E. Hoch for the seasons of at least 1963–1965. These men may have held the steward position, or perhaps the two positions were combined.

In 1958, the Board of Managers increased their salaries another $100 each. In April 1959, the board discussed new boundaries for the Soup Society; however, there was no mention of what these new boundaries might be. In about 1966, the treasurer (presumably Yerkes) sold 439 shares of stock in the Insurance Company of North America. At the same time, he sold off 66 shares of common stock of the Lehigh Coal and Navigation Company. In this same period, the treasurer of the Soup Society cashed in the U.S. Treasury Bonds valued at $7,500 that had been held for a number of years at $2\frac{1}{2}$ percent interest. There is no mention of why all of this cash was needed, since simultaneously the expenses of running the Soup House would appear to be declining. Unless, of course, the salaries of the officers were continuously rising.

In a report to the Board of Managers, Charles F. Weeks, the steward, stated that there had been a decrease in the amount of distributions to local residents, due to the fact that many of them were getting "surplus food" elsewhere. He also stated that there had been only two coal delivery requests for the 1961–62 season. One request had been from a petitioner who requested a half ton of coal as he read from the old sign on the outside of the Soup House. Weeks recommended that the Board of Managers remove the old sign, since it referred to half-ton allotments that were now obsolete. Weeks's report stated: "Many of the families are closely related, parents, children, in-laws, grand-parents, etc., and if coal is given to one, all would ask for it and if refused, the Society would be accused of favoritism which I believe we should avoid."

There were no House Committee reports made from 1956 to 1958, at which point the records stop altogether. What little information exists with regard to the distribution of charity during the period from 1955 to 1981 is shown below in Table 9. These statistics would appear to confirm Charles F. Weeks's statement on the decline of soup distribution. They are not daily statistics, but for the entire seasons; thus, when the Soup House is shown to distribute 2,515 gallons of soup in 1963, this is half as much as it distributed twenty years previously in the early 1940s, and amounts to approximately 34 gallons a day in 1963, compared to 104 gallons a day in 1942.

TABLE 9: Available figures for the period 1955 to 1964, showing the decline of the distribution of soup by the society when compared to the early 1940s (for 1940s, see Tables 7 and 8).

Year	Soup (gals)	Bread (lvs)	Families	Coal (tns)
1955	3,795	1,890	82*	16
1956	4,000	4,600		16
1959	4,883	6,159		17
1960	3,810	6,994	4,755**	13
1961	2,905	3,049	3,380**	
1962	1,790	2,158	2,101**	
1963	2,515	3,079	3,068**	
1964	2,530	2,904	2,691**	

*Persons supplied in three months were 10,531, or 129 per day. The 82 families would appear to be the families that actually registered with the Soup Society.
**These figures would appear to include individuals and families, as there were not thousands of families registered with the Soup House.

While the period from 1965 to 1981 is void of Soup Society monthly minutes, there are receipts that exist for this time period. Receipts from Virnelson's, Bond Bread and Tender Touch bakeries in the years 1975 to 1981 show regular deliveries for the months of the year that the Soup Society was open. Virnelson's Baker, at Thompson and Hutchinson Streets, was delivering twenty to thirty loaves per day from 1975 to 1978, decreasing as the years went on. The bakery had had a business relationship with the Soup House since at least 1950. Bond Bread was delivering between ten and twenty loaves of bread every other day during 1978 and 1979, with Tender Touch picking up the task from 1979 to 1981, at ten to twenty loaves per day when the Soup House was open. The receipts for these companies seem to show that the loaves being ordered were "steak rolls," which were then sliced and given out. The decline of the amount of bread ordered (from twenty to thirty loaves in the late 1970s down to ten to twenty loaves in the early 1980s) also shows the drop of the Soup House's services.

There is also a receipt from John Hall in November 1978. Hall ran a wholesale groceries business in the Olney section of Philadelphia and had billed the Soup House for thirty-four cases of soup, including garden vegetable, chicken noodle, split pea with ham, New England clam chowder, minestrone and tomato with rice. Hall's receipt of 1978 clearly shows that the Soup House had stopped making its own soup.

It was during this questionable period (1959–81) of the Soup Society's history (where hardly any records exist) that the Soup House indeed did stop making soup and started distributing canned soup. In all likelihood, this would have probably happened sometime in the early 1960s, as receipts from Jacobson's Meat Market (235 Wildey Street) still show the society ordering supplies to make soup between 1958 and 1962. A receipt of 1955 has the Soup House ordering five hundred pounds of meat to be supplied during the month of February, along with five hundred pounds of Maine potatoes and one-hundred-pound bags each of coarse barley, baby limas and rice. There were also orders for five hundred pounds of marrow beans, three pounds of paprika and bags of onions, carrots, cabbage, turnips, potatoes, tomatoes and salt, placed in 1955. These were all the ingredients of good healthy soup. Jacobson's had been selling spices, produce and meat to the Soup Society since at least 1940 and there is a cancelled check for him from 1962. Thus, the society was still ordering from him and not serving canned soup yet as late as 1962.

A CHANGING SOUP SOCIETY, 1982–1988

During the period from 1965 to 1981, there is virtually no information whatsoever on the Kensington Soup Society's activities. The absence of business records and ledgers for the Board of Managers monthly meeting minutes was evident when Harriet F. Jablonski took over as secretary in 1991. She also noted that the early years of monthly meeting minutes for the period from 1844 to 1874 were also lacking at that time (1991).

After such a steady and consistent leadership for over one hundred years, the Soup Society started to disintegrate after the post–World War II period. The old guard died off by the middle of the 1950s and a new group of managers came aboard and had to deal with an American institutional landscape that had changed. From a time in the nineteenth century when the poor had been dependent on private institutions and churches for welfare, America had become a society that looked to government agencies to help meet its needs.

When the records of the Kensington Soup Society start to once more note the activities of the society, there were only two Board of Managers members remaining. At a meeting on September 21, 1982, it was recorded that George E. Williams and Thelma Williams were the only managers. Also present at this meeting were a new generation of individuals who would lead the Soup Society. Those individuals were Furman C. Krauter, Herman C. Idler, Betty Quintavalle, Jane H. Molmer, Barbara M. Pomierny, Albert Schenzle, Richard J. Mullen and Benjamin M. Quigg Jr., Esq.

This surviving manager would appear to be the same George E. Williams who was president of the Soup Society in 1965, before the records ceased. Thelma was probably George's wife; thus, the couple over the years took it upon themselves to continue the activities of the Soup House on their own with apparently no outside help (and possibly no record keeping).

The previous secretary, or secretaries, appears to have been neglectful of his duties, since records do not exist for this period from 1965 to 1981. If records did exist, they were not turned over to the new secretary, as was the custom of the society. The last known secretary of the society was the ambitious James R. Anderson Jr., who had resigned the presidency in 1957 to take the remunerative job of secretary.

All of these new individuals, except Quigg, were elected to serve out the remainder of the year as members of the Board of Managers. Later in the year, along with Quigg, they were all elected as the new Board of Managers for the 1982–83 season.

In the minutes of that September 21, 1982 meeting, there is also mention that the "managers instructed the Secretary to send a letter of appreciation to Robert Boyd, Esq., for his efforts in the obtaining of new managers for the Board of Managers of the Kensington Soup Society." This would seem to show that Boyd was enlisted to help recruit individuals for the Board of Managers, as the board had either retired, died out or moved away, and that the society itself was being neglected and on the verge of possibly closing.

This neglect becomes evident when, at the next appointed meeting, the Board of Managers new secretary, Herman C. Idler (a local realtor), found that there was no fire or product liability insurance coverage obtained for the Soup House. It was highly recommended that this coverage be sought out quickly (which it was) and purchased. In order to get the fire insurance, the insurance company required that the society install smoke alarms and recharge the existing fire extinguishers.

The new board was also unsure of where the original property deed to the Soup House might be, but it was found in the safety deposit box that the society kept at First Pennsylvania Company. The list of securities that George E. Williams handed over to the new Board of Managers was investigated and found to be in order, and an outside agency was hired to audit the books of the Soup Society. It was discovered that three different IRS Employer Identification Numbers had been used by the society over the years, so the board contacted the IRS to see which one was correct. New Board of Managers member Richard Mullen was a CPA and put the books of the Soup Society in order by setting up a new accounting system for the treasurer. The new Board of Managers was intent on having the Soup Society in proper working order before getting down to the business of distributing soup.

Whatever happened between 1965 and 1981 is not clear, but what was clear is that the Soup House needed basic repairs and upgrading. A new commercial can opener was quickly purchased and new rubber mats and runners were ordered and installed, but that was just the beginning. Bids were sought for extensive repairs to the roof, gutters and downspouts of the Soup House (which turned out to cost $3,700) and the exterior brick walls needed to be pointed as well, at an estimated cost of $1,550. Later, it was realized that the water pipes coming into the Soup Society from the street were in disrepair and needed to be replaced at a possible cost of $2,200. Some of the windows leaked, several doors had to be repaired and the floor on the first level was beginning to sag.

The entrance hall of the 1036 Crease Street Soup House, circa 1992. *Kensington Soup Society Archives.*

After the resignation of steward Bruce Doebrick in 1984, the Board of Managers decided to do further renovations to the Soup House before hiring a new steward. It is mentioned in the meeting minutes that the whole of the interior of the Soup House needed to be redecorated, a real sign that the Soup House had deteriorated not only outside but inside as well.

The new president, Furman C. Krauter, made new appointments to the House and Finance Committees. He also reconstituted the Real Estate Committee. The new board also authorized that a passbook account be

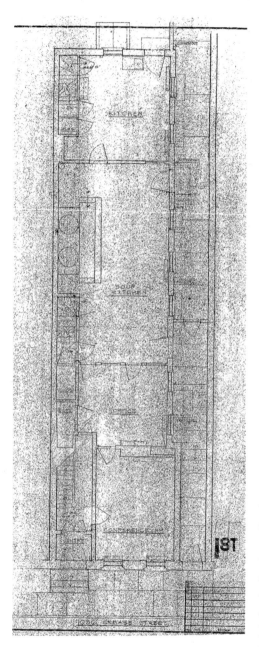

Floor plans for the first floor of the Soup House, drawn by Ally Friends in 1986, after attempts were made to renovate the building. *Kensington Soup Society Archives.*

opened at East Girard Savings Association so that petty cash, dividend checks received, etc., could be easily deposited and available. The assets of the Soup Society remained at First Pennsylvania Company.

At the first full report in November 1983 of the Soup Society's securities since the new board took over, the Soup Society had securities valued at slightly over $200,000, with interest income of slightly more than $16,000. The board decided to hire an outside investment specialist to find ways of investing the society's money for a higher yield.

When the new Board of Managers took over in 1982, the cash-on-hand of the Soup Society was a little over $10,500. After making the necessary repairs to the Soup House and acquiring insurance, etc., the treasury shrank to just under $6,000. However, with some financial movements, the Soup House treasury increased to $24,000 in 1984 and the outlook for the Soup House was improved. By 1986, the expenses of repairing the Soup House had whittled away the treasury to a slight deficit.

Managers of the Soup Society at this time also decided to amend their bylaws so that the Soup Society would qualify for tax-exempt status with the Internal Revenue Service. Apparently, this had never been done, since the society appears to have been operating as a private organization. This status was eventually granted by the IRS on October 18, 1984.

This new Board of Managers also began to meet monthly during the season, rather than at the beginning and at the end of the season, in addition to any special meetings that might be called during the year. After George E. Williams and Thelma Williams attended the first meeting in September 1981, they proceeded to miss the next seven meetings, prompting the Board of Directors in a meeting of April 1983 to inquire whether the Williamses wanted to remain on the board. They might have been content to give way to a younger generation, as George E. Williams had been on the Board of Managers since 1950, a total of thirty-two years. As it turned out, that appears to have been precisely the situation, since the Board of Managers voted to have a "Special Dinner Meeting, November 16, to honor George and Thelma Williams' many years of service."

It was also at this same April 1983 meeting that it was first suggested that James D.B. Weiss Jr. be approached to see if he would like to join the Board of Managers. Weiss did join the board after he attended his first meeting with James Winn in December 1983. Weiss would later become the society's president.

The new Board of Managers resuscitated the Soup Society. A new aspect at this time for the Soup Society, or at least for the first time in the recorded history, the Board of Managers included a number of women. These women were elected managers and not appointees.

Previously, the only women involved in the Soup House's activities had been appointees. Women like Mary Frazier, the wife of Superintendent Robert Frazier, served as stewardesses in the 1880s. Mrs. John Hopkins, presumably the wife of the collector John Hopkins, was appointed as the visitor in 1903–04. Jane Roberts served as superintendent in the 1860s, but again, she was appointed by the board, not elected. Anna Wallace served the Soup Society from 1904 to 1920 in the capacity of visitor, collector, assistant steward and distribution clerk, but all these were appointments by the Board of Managers. There was also the longtime stewardess, Suzie Scherz, who served from 1915 to 1953, but her involvement came as the wife of longtime elected steward Christian Scherz.

Thus, with the elections of 1982, women were finally officially elected to the Board of Managers of the Soup Society. Of course, Thelma Williams appears as one of the managers after the void of 1965 to 1981, but without

One of two fifty-gallon stainless steel kettles of the Soup House. These replaced three twenty-five-gallon copper kettles in the 1980s. *Kensington Soup Society Archives.*

any records for that period, we cannot be sure just how she came to be one of the managers, particularly when her presumed husband, George E. Williams, had previously been the president of the Soup Society.

The 1984–85 season found the Soup Society in search of a new steward. Bruce Doebrick and his wife resigned their positions and decided to move out of the Soup House. After forming a Personnel Committee and advertising for the position through the local churches and newspapers, the Soup Society settled on a local young man by the name of Michael Layton, who accepted the position, but not without requesting that the Soup Society install a shower for his use.

It is unclear why the steward, Bruce Doebrick, decided to resign and move out of the Soup House. It may or may not have had something to do with the new Board of Managers. His reports were brief or, in some cases, possibly not reported at all. The records are not clear, as the minutes only included the February report for the 1982–83 season. It could be that the new board brought new ideas and a sounder system of keeping track of the Soup House's activities and the steward, perhaps being under the previous

Board of Managers, who apparently all but abandoned the Soup House, was not keen on the new ideas and decided to resign. In any event, with the coming of the new steward, Michael Layton, the reports were much more accurate and reported regularly.

Three young women were hired by Layton to help out at the Soup House. Together, they developed a menu that would include a different soup for each day of the week: beef barley, tomato rice, garden vegetable, chef chicken and Manhattan clam chowder. Layton also got approval from the Board of Managers to allow the Soup House to be the gathering place for a local organization that was gathering food to give out over the Christmas holidays. The new Board of Managers and Layton had gotten the Soup House back up and running.

The first reports for the distribution of charity by the new Board of Managers seem to indicate that the Soup House's first full season was somewhat shortened. Reports were recorded only for January and February of 1982–83 season, and even then, the reports were fairly brief, showing only 755 loaves of bread being distributed in January and 573 loaves in February. There is no recording of how much actual soup was given out, but individual servings were 2,596 for January and 2,498 for February. If a serving was a normal cup of soup, then there were approximately 324 gallons of soup distributed in January and 312 gallons in February. This amounted to perhaps one hundred people per day while the Soup House was open.

For the very next season, 1983–84, the Board decided that the new working hours of the Soup House would be "from 11:00 A.M to 1:00 P.M." The Soup House would continue to be open from Monday through Friday with a supplemented portion for weekends. The months that the society opened the Soup House would be expanded to November through March. However, there are reports of distribution only for February, when 220 gallons of soup and 920 loaves of bread were distributed to 798 families, which comprised 2,850 individual servings.

During the 1984–85 season, Layton reported to the Board of Managers that it was "a burden to buy supplies in small quantity and that the Board consider the larger purchases, both from a cost standpoint of view, and a management standpoint of view." His report, as well as the last reports of the previous steward, also showed the soup reported in terms of cans and ounces, which would seem to indicate that the days of buying vegetable and meat ingredients were definitely over and that the Soup House was simply heating and serving canned soup. Table 10 shows Layton's report for the 1984–85 season.

TABLE 10: First full reports of soup distribution by steward Michael Layton after the new Board of Managers took over the Soup House in the early 1980s.

Season 1984–85	Soup (gals)	Bread (lvs)	Families (servings)
November	480	755	705
December	513	598	(2,775)
January	667	756	855
February	395	943	1,032 (4,362)

The 1985–86 season saw the hiring of a new steward, Harry Hoppe. Michael Layton asked to stay on at the Soup House until August 1986, to which the board agreed as a sort of protection for the place. Hoppe lived nearby and did not need lodging at the Soup House. During Layton's tenure as steward, the Soup House had been broken into and an antique clock and other items were stolen, after which grating for the windows was suggested. The 1980s saw a drug epidemic sweeping through Philadelphia's communities; crack cocaine was destroying the lives of the young people in the city, and any unattended building was a potential source of income for thieves. After Layton vacated the place earlier than expected, the Board of Managers began to consider installing a security system. Due to potential security problems, it was reported at a meeting of May 1, 1986, that "James Weiss (one of the Managers) is holding the original papers and special material of the Soup Society" at his home.

It would not be the last time the Soup House was robbed. Two break-ins in 1991 resulted in a number of other items being stolen. One robbery included the theft of the Soup House's computer, seven fire extinguishers, a small two-burner stove, two soup tureens, one small clock, two radios and the kitchen sensor light. The building was also damaged in the process of the burglaries. The vandalized Soup House was forced to close for a day to restore order. The second burglary occurred a month after the first. This time the thieves stole a hand truck, three cases of soup, half a case of toilet paper, half a case of paper towels, a four-inch light fixture, a large wall clock and a toaster oven.

Harry Hoppe, the new steward, grew up a few blocks from the Soup House. In a 1991 interview by a *Philadelphia Daily News* reporter, Hoppe recalled:

Harry Hoppe took over as steward from Michael Layton during the 1985–86 season. *Kensington Soup Society Archives.*

I was raised only a couple blocks from here…I remember coming home from school for lunch in 1930, and my mother would give me a dime and a little kettle. And I'd pick up the soup and bread…During the Depression; there were hundreds of families using the soup kitchen…The lines went out the door and all the way around the block. There were four people handing out numbers and three people giving out soup.

Hoppe explained to the *Daily News* reporter the system of distributing the soup; it hadn't changed much over the years. According to the reporter:

Anyone living within the boundaries of Fishtown you can register—there was no means test, no financial questions asked. The number of the people in the family is listed, and each family is given an identification number. Clients would arrive between 11 a.m. and 1 p.m. They give Hoppe their I.D. numbers. He hands out cards bearing numbers corresponding to the number of people in the family. The card is handed to the person dishing out soup from huge, commercial-size cauldrons. The number "Four" means four ladles of soup and 12 slices of white bread.

Steward Harry Hoppe and assistant Bill Wallace preparing for the opening of the Soup House, 1992. *Kensington Soup Society Archives.*

While Harry Hoppe had seen many things in his day, none was more astonishing than the day he was assaulted inside the Soup House. In March 1992, an individual came into the Soup House. Harry noticed that the container the fellow wanted his soup put into was dirty. After telling the man that he could not give him soup in a dirty container, the man "took the container and spit in it and showed it to me—and said now it is clean."

The man then became rather loud and boisterous. A man in line told the man to quiet down and the irate toad proceeded to club the man over the head with a stick he had. When Harry approached the man, the man took a swing at Harry. Other men got involved and chased the man down Crease Street. Needless to say, that man was never served soup again.

THE DECLINE OF THE DISTRIBUTION OF SOUP

To really see what the Soup House now meant to the community, and how much less the community relied on the Soup House for charity, we only need to review statistics for some of the years of the Soup House. During World

War I, the Great Depression and World War II, the Soup House provided much more to the needs of the community. But now, with the advent of government assistance programs, the Soup House was becoming more of an outmoded charity, an antique institution whose purpose and mission had become obsolete due to the various government programs that had sprung up since the New Deal of the 1930s. Public assistance, food stamps, the WIC program, Social Security, SSI and the like have all cut into the purpose of the Soup Society. This fact is shown by the distribution statistics recorded in Table 11.

TABLE 11: Soup distribution statistics over the years illustrating the decline of the Soup House's activities as government assistance programs became available.

Years	Average Gallons of Soup Served Yearly
1860–65	12,000*
1876–79	13,094
1914–18	14,668
1925–29	7,302
1930–34	12,110
1935–39	7,011
1940–45	5,086
1946–52	2,414
1955–64	3,202*
1984–87	1,962*
1990–96	1,181

*These figures are calculated approximations from some available statistics for these time periods.

The amount of soup being distributed per year by the Soup Society had been declining since World War I, even as the population of Philadelphia had been rising. Philadelphia's population peeked in the 1950s with two million people, but by that point the government had stepped in with a whole host of subsidized programs to help the poor, which led to decline in the need for soup distribution.

For a better part of the nineteenth century, the Soup Society appears to have given out on a yearly basis well over twelve thousand gallons of soup. The high point came during World War I (1914–18), when the total amount of soup distributed was actually greater than the amount given out annually during the Great Depression. As the Depression bottomed out and the federal government phased in the public assistance programs, the decline of soup distribution by the Soup House began, so much so that by the 1990s, the distribution decreased by a whopping 92 percent of what it had been seventy years earlier.

The 1984–85 figures are actually misleading and overstate the distribution, since at that point the reports indicate the average serving of soup between twenty and twenty-three ounces. Prior to the 1950s, the reports were usually in pints (or sixteen-ounce increments), which seemed to be the standard serving size. Going back further to the latter parts of the nineteenth century, we can calculate the amount of soup served divided by the people served, and we find the servings tended to be one cup, or eight ounces. So, while the number of gallons of soup distributed decreased dramatically, they are still somewhat misleading, due to the large proportions given out when compared with previous years.

In the 1990s, the Soup House was on average distributing 1,181 gallons of soup per season. A season was twenty-four weeks from October through

A 1992 five-day menu of the Soup House: Monday—garden vegetable, Tuesday—tomato, Wednesday—beef barley, Thursday—chicken noodle and Friday—clam chowder. *Kensington Soup Society Archives.*

March, later shortened in 1994 to twenty-two weeks in order to try to reign in the deficit the Soup House was running. During 1995–96, the Soup House distributed 1,014 gallons of soup, an average of 46 gallons per week, or a little over 9 gallons per day. This was a far cry from the time when it would regularly serve 125 gallons per day in 1866, or even the 90 to 100 gallons per day back in the 1920s.

By the 1987–88 season, the expense of running the Soup House was approaching $22,000 per year. With income of approximately $20,000 per year, the Soup Society was beginning to run a deficit, while cutting into its endowments. Its investments were not doing as well as members had hoped. While the budget could be temporarily manipulated and balanced, there was no money for long-term maintenance and upkeep of the Soup House.

New Beginnings and Mission, 1990–2008

By the 1989–90 season, President Furman Krauter had retired and the new president, James D.B. Weiss Jr., had been elected. Weiss continued to serve as president until recently. He would have to deal with the problem of Campbell Soup Company's discontinuance of its charity, as well as the increasing price of soup. The annual cost of soup was $3,000 more in 1992 than the previous year.

During this period, the Soup Society also began grooming a young man by the name of Keith A. Dailey as its future treasurer. Dailey was a native Fishtowner from Montgomery Avenue and a descendant of the Birely family, one of the original founding families of the Kensington Soup Society. He was studying to become a CPA. The Board of Managers accommodated Dailey and even agreed to switch its meetings to evenings when he was not attending school. Dailey also took up lodgings at the Soup House, not only renovating the living quarters but also giving the Soup Society a much-needed physical presence on the property when it was not in service. Burglaries continued to be a potential problem for the Soup House. It was suggested by the Board of Managers that Dailey work in conjunction with acting treasurer Rich Mullen so that Dailey could learn the books of the Soup House and be able to take over the duties of treasurer full time, which he eventually did.

In addition to looking for new sources of income, the Board of Managers also reviewed the quality of the food being distributed at the Soup House. The board suggested that it would be appropriate to have a nutrition expert

Kensington Soup Society Board of Managers, 1992. *Kensington Soup Society Archives.*

visit the Soup House to inspect its operation, "since there are so many mistakes in the world with food today."

In a *Philadelphia Daily News* article of March 11, 1991, it was stated that the home-cooked soup of the Soup House had ceased about "forty years ago" and that it had been serving Campbell's soup ever since. The interviewee's memory was slightly off, as receipts exist in the Soup Society archives that show it was still making its own soup into the early 1960s. However, the Campbell Soup Company had made regular donations of cases of soup (up to five hundred cases a season in some instances), but discontinued donations starting in the 1991–92 season. The same article goes on to state that the Kensington Soup Society was the only soup society that was still dispensing soup. All the others had closed or, as in the case of the Spring Garden Soup Society, had become a philanthropic organization, which actually helped to financially support the Kensington Soup Society.

In September 1992, the first meeting was held by the Soup Society's Board of Managers on the issue of the 150th anniversary of the society. A menu of pepper pot and snapper soup was discussed, along with coordinating the Soup Society's 150th anniversary with First Presbyterian Church of Kensington's 180th anniversary. It was noted in the minutes of a Board of Managers meeting held in January 1994 that the Board of Managers' "predecessors did not wish any notoriety for their good works, believing the main purpose of the Soup Society was to serve those in need, nothing more. However, Jim Weiss has been working on a few ideas and will keep us advised."

At this point in the Soup Society's operations, members had begun to look beyond their investments and charitable donations and formulated a proposal for potential grants, in addition to a new stockbroker and better management of the treasury. Assistant treasurer Richard Mullen suggested that the Soup Society stay within a $16,000 operating budget. Thus, by the year 1994, the Soup House was forced to operate for only twenty-two weeks instead of twenty-four.

It was eventually decided that in lieu of an anniversary celebration, the society would have an open house at the Soup House on April 23, 1994, "with all members present, refreshments will be served, and this would be an opportune time to honor the members (Richard Mullen, Jane Molmer, Barbara Pomierny, and Margaret McAvinue) who recently retired/resigned."

The 150th anniversary celebration. *Left to right*: Betty Quintavalle, James Winn and Harriet Jablonski, 1994. *Kensington Soup Society Archives*.

With the retirement of four Board of Managers members, the Soup Society began looking for replacements. It found them in Judge William J. Lederer, Robin Schimpf (a journalist for the local newspaper), Ann Richardson and John F. Szymanski. The Soup Society now had a complete ten-member voting Board of Managers.

By the mid-1990s, the Soup Society had begun to improve its financial position. After shortening its season by two weeks, finding a new stockbroker to handle its investments and with some excellent bookkeeping by the treasurer, the society was starting to see increased assets rather than continuing deficits. However, most of the money realized went right back into the never-ending repairs on the Soup House. Another problem the Soup Society faced, which presumably was a good one, was the fact that fewer and fewer people needed its services, leaving the Board of Managers with little to do.

In 1997, Harriet Jablonski, the secretary of the Board of Managers, felt it necessary to call a meeting due to the fact that the society had not met as a board for almost nine months. In a letter dated July 1997 and addressed to the Board of Managers, Jablonski stated, "Our members have not met formally at a meeting since the last meeting November 7, 1996…as your Secretary, I believe it is important to set a date for our meeting prior to opening our kitchen."

Jablonski set the date for October 2, 1997, but never made the meeting herself. She moved from Philadelphia in September 1997, resigning in a letter dated August 22, 1997, and handing all of the secretary's material (the ledgers of monthly meeting minutes) on to the treasurer, Keith A. Dailey.

The Kensington Soup Society by the turn of the century found itself in a position similar to that of the society in 1980–81, when George and Thelma Williams ran the organization by themselves. The energized Board of Managers, recruited by Robert Boyd in 1981–82, which helped renovate the Soup House and put it back on a sound financial footing in the 1980s, was now (twenty years later) retiring, moving away or in some cases even dying. President James D.B. Weiss Jr., not in good health, retired to Penn Home. By the 2005–06 season, the board had become almost non-functioning. The energy that the Board of Managers of previous years had brought to the society was hard to sustain, and there was no equivalent to a Robert Boyd or James D.B. Weiss Jr. to recruit a new board.

By the 2000–01 season, the Soup Society was down to distributing approximately twenty-five large twenty-six-ounce family-size cans of soup. This amount continued to decrease until the society found itself, for the

2006–07 season, heating up only a crock pot of soup as a way to at least say that it was open. The fact that there were fewer and fewer residents seeking the society's charity allowed the board the ability to cease meeting on a regular basis. The only real issue that the board constantly faced was how to care for the physical structure of the Soup House that again began needing repairs.

Keith A. Dailey, the society's treasurer, continued to play a role in the Soup Society. Dailey's father Thomas and brothers Daniel and David also helped to care for the Soup House, along with President James D.B. Weiss Jr., who, while getting up in years and not in good health, still provided guidance. Finally, after several extremely slow seasons, the remaining Board of Managers made the heartbreaking decision to close the Soup House for the 2007–08 season, plan a new mission for the society and sell the financially draining Soup House.

After much deliberation and discussion on the topic, it was decided that the new mission of the Kensington Soup Society would be one of a philanthropic society that would financially support local institutions in the Fishtown and Kensington neighborhoods. The idea was mirrored after the Spring Garden Soup Society. Founded in 1853, the Spring Garden Society had ceased functioning as a soup kitchen in 1932. After the closing of its soup house, Spring Garden began to provide direct distribution of food and fuel to people's homes. As circumstances changed, the society's mission changed and it began to offer financial support to Philadelphia institutions that provide food services to residents of the city.

The Kensington Soup Society's new mission will not only help to preserve itself, but its financial support of neighborhood institutions like Penn Home and Palmer Cemetery will hopefully ensure that these organizations continue on as well. Strangely enough, 164 years from the time of the society's founding, the Dailey family, descendants of the Birelys, one of the founding families of the Kensington Soup Society, was put into the odd position of being the ones to close the door on the Soup House, but at the same time start a new chapter in the history of the Kensington Soup Society.

With this new mission of the Soup Society starts another chapter in its long history. One can only hope, recalling the Soup House prayer, and wish them success:

> *Heavenly Father we come to you tonight as a Board,*
> *And also as individuals. We ask that our talents,*
> *However many or few, be used to carry on the work of*

The Soup Society in an orderly fashion. Guide us
In this effort. Bless those who operate the kitchen,
All who enter in for food. May they realize from
Whence it comes. Not from those who serve, or the
Board, but from thee O'Lord, who planted the seed
In hearts of good people many years ago. May we
Consider it a privilege to carry on their works
In your Name. Amen.
—composed by Betty Quintavalle in 1992 as the opening prayer
for Kensington Soup Society's Board of Managers meetings

Visit us at
www.historypress.net